The Cambridge Manuals of Science and
Literature

THE HISTORICAL GROWTH OF THE
ENGLISH PARISH CHURCH

St Benet's, Cambridge: west tower from N.W.

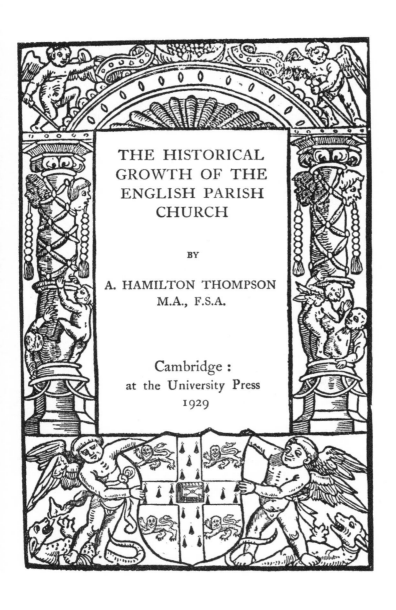

THE HISTORICAL GROWTH OF THE ENGLISH PARISH CHURCH

BY

A. HAMILTON THOMPSON
M.A., F.S.A.

Cambridge:
at the University Press
1929

CAMBRIDGE UNIVERSITY PRESS
Cambridge, New York, Melbourne, Madrid, Cape Town,
Singapore, São Paulo, Delhi, Tokyo, Mexico City

Cambridge University Press
The Edinburgh Building, Cambridge CB2 8RU, UK

Published in the United States of America by Cambridge University Press, New York

www.cambridge.org
Information on this title: www.cambridge.org/9781107605787

© Cambridge University Press 1913

First published 1913
First paperback edition 2011

A catalogue record for this publication is available from the British library

ISBN 978-1-107-60578-7 Paperback

*With the exception of the coat of arms at
the foot, the design on the title page is a
reproduction of one used by the earliest known
Cambridge printer, John Siberch, 1521*

PREFACE

THIS small book is intended to be a companion and complement to the writer's book in the same series on *The Ground Plan of the English Parish Church*. In that book the growth of the ground plan is treated with necessarily scanty reference to the circumstances to which, directly or indirectly, that growth is due. Some attempt is made in the present volume to supply an account of the historical conditions amid which our parish churches were built, to say something of the builders, and to remove the popular idea, still current even among educated people, that our architecture is mainly due to the profuse benefactions of the religious orders. A special chapter on chantry foundations, which played so large a part in the life of the later middle ages, follows the general historical chapter. The western tower, the porch, and the chancel are then described with more fulness than was possible in the description of the ground plan ; and the decoration and furniture of the various parts of the church are treated in the closing chapter.

The writer returns thanks for much help to his wife, to whom a sketch and the plans in the book, except that of Burford, are due ; to the Rev. J. C. Cox, LL.D., F.S.A., and to the Rev. R. M. Serjeantson, M.A., F.S.A., who have read through his proofs, and provided him with many useful suggestions ; to the editor of the *Archaeological Journal*, for the use of the plan of Burford church; and to Messrs C. C. Hodges, J. P. Gibson, F.S.A., E. Kennerell, and A. J. Loughton, for the loan of photographs.

A. H. T.

April, 1911.

NOTE TO SECOND EDITION

A few alterations have been made in the present edition. The writer desires to thank correspondents for numerous suggestions, some of which have been adopted. A special word of gratitude is due to Dr Cox and to Mr W. H. St John Hope, Litt.D., D.C.L., for valuable hints.

CONTENTS

CHAPTER I

THE HISTORICAL DEVELOPMENT OF THE PARISH CHURCH

SECTION   PAGE
1. Early parish churches in England   1
2. The monastic missionary settlements : church-building
    on private estates   3
3. The Danish invasions and the monastic revival   .   .   5
4. German influence on pre-Conquest architecture   .   6
5. Influence of the Normans on the architecture of parish
    churches   7
6. The parish church at the Norman conquest   .   .   10
7. Appropriation of churches to monasteries : ordination
    of vicarages   11
8. Relation of monastic owners to the fabrics of churches   13
9. The builders of medieval parish churches .   .   .   15
10. The parish church and its rectors   .   .   .   17
11. Disadvantages of pluralism and litigation .   .   .   18
12. Growth of the chantry system   20
13. Chantry chapels at Beckingham, Lincolnshire   .   .   21
14. Summary   22

CHAPTER II

THE CHANTRY CHAPEL IN THE PARISH CHURCH

15. Chantries and colleges of chantry priests .   .   .   24
16. Foundation of chantry colleges   27
17. Parochial chapels   29

SECTION		PAGE
18.	Religious and trade guilds	30
19, 20.	The chantry chapel: its influence on the church plan	33
21.	Chancels of collegiate churches	37
22.	St John Baptist's, Cirencester	39
23.	Chesterfield and Scarborough; charnel chapels . .	41
24.	Burford church, Oxon	42
25.	St Michael's and Holy Trinity, Coventry . . .	45
26.	Importance of the work of lay benefactors . . .	48

CHAPTER III

THE TOWER, THE PORCH, AND THE CHANCEL

27.	Subject of the chapter	51
28.	The western tower before the Conquest . . .	53
29.	Survival of the older type of tower after the Conquest .	56
30.	Architectural development of the tower . . .	59
31.	The spire	60
32.	The tower of the later middle ages : its relation to the clerestory of the nave	62
33.	Western doorways and porches	65
34.	Side doorways of the church	67
35.	The porch: altars in porches	68
36.	Chambers above porches	71
37.	Altars in towers: habitations in connexion with churches	73
38.	Variety of position of the tower	75
39.	The chancel arch	76
40.	Enlargement of the chancel and architectural treatment	78
41.	Fourteenth century chancels in Yorkshire and the northern midlands	80

CONTENTS

SECTION   PAGE

42. Decline of chancel building in the fifteenth century:
the laity and the nave 85
43. Sacristies 88
44. Squints, priests' doors, low side windows . . . 90
45. Crypts and bone-holes 95

CHAPTER IV

THE FURNITURE OF A MEDIEVAL PARISH CHURCH:
CONCLUSION

46. Remains of medieval decorations 98
47. Mural paintings 98
48. Stained glass 102
49. Coloured furniture of stone and wood . . . 105
50. Furniture of the nave and aisles: font and benches . 106
51. Chapels in aisles 109
52. Pulpits, galleries, etc. 110
53. The rood screen 112
54. The rood loft and beam 116
55. Quire stalls and lectern 117
56. Levels of the chancel 119
57. The altar and its furniture 120
58. Piscina, sedilia, and almeries 122
59. The Easter sepulchre 124
60. Exceptional furniture 128
61. Parish churches after the Reformation . . . 129
62. Later parish churches 130
63. Post-reformation work and modern restoration . . 131

Bibliography 134
Index 137

LIST OF ILLUSTRATIONS

St Benet's, Cambridge: west tower from N.W. *Frontispiece*

PAGE

Sketch of Hallaton, chantry chapel in S. aisle . . . 25
Plan of Cirencester Church 40
Plan of Burford Church 43
Plan of St Michael's Church, Coventry 46
Plan of Holy Trinity Church, Coventry 47
Norton, Co. Durham: Saxon central tower, with transept 52
Carlton-in-Lindrick, Notts: west tower 57
Tickhill, Yorkshire: general view from S.E., shewing clere-
    story, western tower and projecting eastern chapel . 63
St Mary's, Beverley: south porch 69
Cirencester: south porch 72
Patrington: north side of chancel and vestry . . 83
Walpole St Peter: from S.E. 86
Wensley: chancel, with low side window, from S.E. 91
St Mary Redcliffe, Bristol: from S.E. 95
Patrington: interior, looking across nave from S. transept 99
Well, Yorkshire: font cover 107
Banwell, Somerset: rood screen 113
Hawton, Notts: Easter sepulchre 125

CHAPTER I

THE HISTORICAL DEVELOPMENT OF THE PARISH CHURCH

§ 1. The early history of the English parish church is obscure, owing to the fact that architectural remains of the earliest fabrics are somewhat scanty, and that their actual date still affords ground for dispute. The episcopal constitution of the Romano-British church is not fully known ; but it is probable that, as in Gaul, every considerable centre of population possessed within its walls a church, which followed the 'basilican' arrangement common to the Christian churches of the Roman empire. But while, on the continent of Europe, the ecclesiastical history of the chief provincial capitals remained unbroken, and the great cathedrals of the middle ages rose upon sites which had been, from the establishment of Christianity in the empire, the centres of the religious life of Roman cities, the continuous history of church-building in England was broken by the relapse into

heathenism which followed the victorious invasions
of the Saxons. The history of church architecture
begins again with the coming of St Augustine in
597 A.D. Of churches which may reasonably be said
to have been built as an immediate result of his
mission, there are several remains in Kent ; and the
famous church of St Martin at Canterbury is probably
in large part the building which he and his companions
used for their first services. There is more than one
theory as to the original extent of the church ; but
there can be little doubt that the western part of the
chancel, the south wall of which is built of Roman
brick, is of Augustine's time. Bede tells us that
Augustine found an earlier church, built during the
Roman occupation, on this site or on a site closely
corresponding to it. It is safe to assume that he
repaired this building, and spared all that he could of
its materials. Apart from the Kentish churches there
remains, on the remote part of the Essex coast, a
building known as St Peter's on the Wall, which
appears to be connected architecturally with the
Kentish group. Its history cannot be traced back
earlier than about 653 A.D., when St Cedd was sent
from Northumbria to preach to the East Saxons.
One of his two chief missionary centres was the
Roman city of Othona, then known as Ythanceaster,
at the mouth of the Blackwater. Here he ordained
and baptized : he also, says Bede, built churches in

several places. St Peter's on the Wall, now long
disused, stands on the site of the eastern gateway
of Othona, and is largely built of re-used Roman
material. It presents difficulties of site and plan
which forbid us to connect it positively with St
Cedd ; but there is a high probability that it is his
church, while, in point of plan, it is too closely allied
to the Kentish group to admit of a doubt as to its
connexion with those churches. The actual way in
which the connexion came about is, however, a
difficult problem to solve.

§ 2. There is much uncertainty with regard
to the chronology of pre-Conquest architecture in
England. From the actual masonry of the buildings it
is difficult to gather much information. Saxon builders shewed little architectural skill : their methods
were unprogressive; and the chief criterion by which
we may estimate any degree of progress in their
work is found in their efforts to develop the ground
plan of their churches. The course of architectural
evolution between the coming of St Augustine and
the Norman conquest suffered more than one serious
check. The later part of the seventh century, the
age of Wilfrid and archbishop Theodore, was an
epoch during which ecclesiastical art flourished.
It is now that we arrive at the beginning of the
history of the parish church as distinguished from the
monastic missionary settlement of early Saxon times.

The churches which Augustine and his companions had founded at Canterbury and Rochester were churches of monasteries, established as missionary centres in a heathen kingdom.   The work of evangelisation was carried on for a century afterwards by the agency of monastic communities.   The churches of Benedict Biscop at Monkwearmouth and Jarrow, Wilfrid's churches at Hexham and Ripon, the Mercian churches of Peterborough and Brixworth, were all churches of monks.   But, as Christianity grew in the Saxon kingdoms, churches were naturally multiplied. Wilfrid himself was a large land-owner in Mercia, and may be credited with the building of churches upon his lands : the foundation of the monastery of Brixworth and the church of Barnack may be attributed to his influence.   His example would be followed by others ; and we shall not be far wrong if we look upon the private estate of Saxon times as identical with the early parish.   Owners of large estates built churches upon their property ; and undoubtedly the growth of church-building on private lands led to that organisation of the ecclesiastical system in England, which was the great work of Theodore's episcopate.   During this period, the church plan was founded upon a compromise ; but continental influence, if modified by contact with Celtic traditions, was strong ; and this influence came from Italy through the channel of the Gallican church.

§ 3. When Wilfrid died in 709 A.D., the age of religious and artistic activity was already passing. The power of Northumbria was declining; and the record of the next hundred years is one of quarrels between the various tribal kings of Britain. At the end of the eighth century the Northmen appeared on the Northumbrian coast. Significant features of their activity were the destruction of the church of Lindisfarne and the sack of the monastery at Wearmouth. During the next fifty years, while the kingdom of Wessex was rising to the front place in English affairs, the incursions of the Danes became more constant. In 851 A.D. a Danish army took up its winter quarters in England. From Thanet and Sheppey the Northmen extended their ravages over the whole east coast. The army which defeated the East Anglian levies at Thetford in 870 marked its progress across Mercia and East Anglia by the destruction of monasteries, chief among them the abbey of Peterborough. During the next hundred years, under the constant pressure of Danish invasion, little or no church-building can have been done; and it is likely that, for a long time before 870, little progress had been made. In 958 or 959 Edgar the Peaceable succeeded to the throne of Wessex and became master of the whole of England. During his reign, which lasted till 975, the great ecclesiastics who rose to influence at his court, Dunstan, Oswald and Ethelwold, busied themselves with the re-establishment of monasticism in England, and the rebuilding of churches. The activity of Oswald in Worcestershire, Gloucestershire, and at Ramsey in Huntingdonshire, of Ethelwold at Winchester, Ely and Peterborough, shews how widespread was the area of the destruction wrought by the Danes. This period of revival lasted until the beginning of the eleventh century. The Danish conquest under the heathen Swegen brought more destruction with it, and although Cnut restored the churches which his father had destroyed, it was probably not until the accession of Edward the Confessor in 1042 that another era of church-building began in earnest.

§ 4. During the religious revival under Dunstan and his fellow prelates, the reformers looked once more to the continent for inspiration. Gaul, however, was no longer a possible source. Between England and the French kingdom which was rising on the ruins of the Neustrian monarchy, lay the Danelaw of Gaul, the province of Normandy. Although the abbey of Fleury on the Loire had a strong influence on the revival, intercourse was less restricted with the neighbourhood of the Rhine, where the Austrasian kingdom pursued its existence under the powerful sway of the Saxon emperors who had superseded the house of Charles the Great. It was from monasteries in this district that the restoration

of the religious life in England was most powerfully
helped ; and with such help, came inevitably architectural influence.   If we are to look anywhere for
the immediate origin of such well-known features of
pre-Conquest architectural detail as "long-and-short"
work or strip-work, it is to be found in the early
religious buildings of the Rhine provinces.   Their ulti-
mate origin was, no doubt, Italian ; but during this
period, English building indicates no such close com-
munication with original sources as existed during
the period of Gallo-Roman influence.   The era of
German influence lasted but a short time, and examples of it, though familiar from the peculiar details
of their masonry, are comparatively few.   The builders
of the period immediately preceding the Conquest
seem to have been thrown more upon their own
resources, and to have abandoned German details
gradually in favour of a more simple fashion of building.   Certain German features, however, which had
been imperfectly developed during the period of revival, persisted in their work; and the closest parallels
to the English towers of the eleventh century, so
common in Lincolnshire and parts of Yorkshire, are
to be seen in western Germany, and in that part of
Italy where German influence was most powerful.

§ 5.   The development of Norman architecture in
England was due to the increasing skill in construction which followed the Conquest.   For the building

of the larger churches, foreign prelates relied on the help of Norman masons, trained in artistic methods far in advance of those which Saxon builders had learned to use. The great aisled churches of the monasteries, Durham, Winchester, Norwich, or Gloucester, planned and built under the superintendence of men who were in close touch with the contemporary art of Normandy, led the way, and provided patterns of architecture which could not fail to exercise an influence upon the smaller churches of the country. In the early parish churches of the Norman period, we cannot expect to find this influence strongly marked. Local masons had little opportunity of acquaintance with the more advanced craftsmanship of the Normans until some large cathedral or abbey church rose in their neighbourhood, and supplied them with a model. Even then their imitation would be rough and uncertain, until practice made perfect their first attempts. The model would also provide them with a plan far beyond the requirements of a parish church, where a single priest served a limited congregation. There was no need of the provision of a large quire or of a number of separate altars : the ritual necessaries were all of the simplest kind. The old plan therefore sufficed in most instances. It is in the masonry that we notice the earliest introduction of modifications and improvements. The thin Saxon walling gives place to more massive construction :

walls composed of a rubble core with facings of
dressed stone take the place of the rubble masonry
with through-stone quoins and dressings of the later
Saxon period. The recessing of the arch, with shafts in
its jambs, becomes gradually understood : the begin-
nings of the practice were rough and unintelligent,
and it was not without difficulty that the local builder
learned the structural use of jamb-shafts as supporting and corresponding to the orders of the arch above.
Our country churches supply many instances of this
faltering treatment of new motives. Here and there
it is possible to trace the direct influence of some
large Norman building on the work of the country
mason.   At Branston, four miles south-east of
Lincoln, the western tower of the church belongs to
the class which is common in the neighbourhood—a
class whose origin is earlier than the introduction
of Norman influence.   Its masonry has several
characteristics of the type known as Saxon. But
the high arch of its western doorway, and the small
arcades which have been introduced, on either side
of the doorway, in the face of the tower, shew very
clearly that its builder had seen Norman work, and
was attempting, roughly, but not without success, to
copy it. Further, the arch of its doorway, and the
tall shafts, with crocketed capitals, which support it,
are beyond doubt closely imitated from the lower
arches of the Norman west front of Lincoln minster.

As the Norman church at Lincoln was consecrated in
1092, the tower at Branston can hardly be earlier
than that date, and may be several years later. Such
examples as this shew that there is still much to
discover with regard to the chronology of the later
Saxon architecture, and that the grasp of new methods
by native builders was acquired very gradually.

§ 6. We know, from the indications with respect
to certain counties supplied by Domesday Book, that
in 1086 the number of parish churches in England
corresponded closely to the number which existed
until the comparatively modern sub-division of
parishes. Domesday was not intended to be a
directory or clergy list; and the return of the
churches existing upon manors depended upon the
view which its individual compilers took of their
duties. We have seen that the earliest English
churches were monastic centres of missionary influence, built on land granted by wealthy converts
to Christianity. The revival at the end of the tenth
century was also monastic. But, after the age of
Dunstan, the monastic ideal suffered an eclipse. The
parish churches of the later Saxon age, although
many of them had been granted to, and remained
the property of monasteries, were for the most part,
if not entirely, served by secular priests who were
under no monastic obligation. The parish was
co-extensive, so far as we can tell, with the estate

of the Saxon landlord : in most cases the church was his property, the appointment of the priest lay in his hands, and the church and its advowson passed to the Norman land-owner who superseded him.

§ 7. With the Norman conquest came a great revival of monastic life. The conquerors founded and heaped benefactions on new monasteries, or enlarged the possessions of Norman abbeys by granting them new estates in England. Many manors and more churches thus became the property of religious houses ; and, where the property of a benefactor was widely scattered, a monastery might acquire a number of churches in many different counties. Thus the church of Kirkby in Malhamdale, in west Yorkshire, became the property of the abbey of West Dereham, in Norfolk ; while a moiety of the tithes of Gisburn, in the same neighbourhood, belonged to the nuns of Stainfield, near Lincoln. These gifts, in the first instance, depended entirely on the free will of pious benefactors. The monasteries were naturally expected to present suitable priests to the churches ; but this was left to their discretion. The logical result of these unconditional benefactions was that, as time went on, many churches were totally appropriated by monasteries : the income from the tithes, which should have served for the support of parish priests, was absorbed by the religious proprietors. Bishops recognised the evil ; and towards the

beginning of the thirteenth century steps were taken
to check the control of monasteries over their subject
churches.   Archbishop Geoffrey Plantagenet in 1205
allowed the abbey of West Dereham to appropriate
the fruits of the church of Kirkby in Malhamdale,
but required them to reserve a stipend of ten marks
yearly for a vicar.   Such ordinations of vicarages
became common within the next few years ; and the
great feature of the episcopate of Hugh of Wells,
bishop of Lincoln 1209–35, was the provision of
vicars, not monks, but secular priests with sufficient
stipends, in the appropriated churches of his huge
diocese.   The monastery was usually allowed to take
the greater tithes, *i.e.* the tithes of corn, for itself, the
smaller tithes, or a sum in commutation of them,
being reserved to the vicar.   The study of episcopal
registers shews that these provisions were sometimes
evaded ; and anyone who has made out lists of vicars
of appropriated churches knows that frequently long
gaps occur, in which it is probable that the monastery
allowed the presentation to lapse unchecked ; but
the ordination of vicarages was in great measure a
cure for the evil.   However, during the thirteenth
century, laymen still continued to present religious
bodies with large gifts of property.   The inroads
which these benefactions began to make upon estates
held in chief of the king were a menace to royal
power.   In order to provide a regular restraint upon

the growth of ecclesiastical property, the statute of
mortmain was passed in 1279. As a consequence of
this measure, any man who wished to alienate land
or churches to a religious corporation, was required
to apply for royal letters patent. If it were found
by inquisition that the property could be alienated
without prejudice to the king or the lord from whom
the fee was immediately held, the licence was granted;
and, if a church formed part of the property, the
religious corporation was allowed to appropriate it
by the grant of a further licence, the ordination of a
vicarage being left to the decree of the bishop. It
need hardly be said that a very large number of
churches remained all through the middle ages in the
hands of private patrons, and that by no means all
churches granted to monasteries were appropriated
by them. Of the arrangements for these unappropriated rectories more will be said later. The connexion of the parish churches with the monasteries
is of great importance, however, for our present
purpose.

§ 8. As so many churches belonged to monasteries, it is constantly assumed that the monasteries,
especially during Norman times, provided parish
churches at their own expense. Thus the splendid
series of churches in south Lincolnshire, on the road
from Sutton Bridge to Spalding, is said, without
historical foundation, to have been produced by

rivalry in church-building between Croyland abbey
and other monasteries. It is true that, as at Spalding
in 1284, the religious house would probably contribute
a certain amount to the building or rebuilding of an
appropriated church, but that amount would be
limited, and the parishioners would be left to provide
the rest according to their means.   When vicarages
were ordained, the repair of the chancel, the rector's
peculiar property, was usually left to the monastery
as rector; but we often find that a special stipulation
was made by which part of the repairs even of this
portion of the church devolved upon the vicar, and
that sometimes his stipend was so arranged as to free
the monastery of this obligation altogether.   A monastery naturally regarded the fruits of a church as
an addition to its own income.   The most that could
be expected of it would be that it would employ a
reasonable part of the profits in keeping the fabric
in order.   If the monastery owned the manor as well
as the advowson, it probably, and here and there un-
mistakably, did more for the fabric of the parish
church. But these fabrics were in most cases existing
when the monasteries took seisin of the advowsons
of the churches in question.   When appropriation
followed, the enrichment of the monastery, not the
enlargement of the building, was the end in view ;
and the plea made by the monastery in dealing with
the bishop over appropriations, was invariably one

of poverty. When a church, then, was rebuilt or enlarged, the money came for the most part from parishioners, the monastery supplying its proportion, not without a view to strict economy.

§ 9. Further, the builders were generally, it may be assumed, local masons. We have seen an indication of this at Branston, where the builder grafted imitative detail in a new style upon his own old-fashioned work. The splendid development of many twelfth century parish churches is no argument against their local origin. Architectural enthusiasm in the middle ages was a possession of the people generally : it was not confined to a limited and privileged body. The large monastery or cathedral churches in every neighbourhood were sources of inspiration to the builders of the parish churches : details were copied, and methods of construction were learned from them, and the structural progress which took place in them had a constant influence upon the architectural improvement of the less important buildings. Here and there, perhaps, a mason, who had taken part in the building of one of the greater churches, would be called into consultation for the design of a parish church ; and this, as years went by, would become more common. It should be noted that in the middle ages the builder was not a mere instrument to carry out the designs of an architect. He himself, the master mason of the work, was

the architect.   His training lay, not in the draughts-
manship of an architect's office, but in practical
working with mallet and chisel.   Thus, during at any
rate the earlier part of the middle ages, design was in
no small degree a matter of instinct.   Architecture
was a popular, democratic art, in which the instinctive
faculties became trained to a high pitch.   The
individual mason was allowed free play for his
talent; and the result was that constant variety of
design and detail, that continual movement and
progress, those forward steps or that conservative
hesitation in the art of different districts, which are
the eternal attraction of medieval architecture.   One
feature of the instinctive faculty of design in the
builder was that he did much of his work by eye
alone.   He must have made some rough measure-
ments for the setting out of his buildings; but he
was not always provided with a plan or elevations.
Even in our larger churches, his work was sometimes
left to his own judgment.   The western transept at
Lincoln, for example, can hardly have been built with
much forethought.   Each set of masons employed
upon it seems to have been left to its own devices:
accurate spacing was entirely neglected, and the
connexion between the different parts of the design
was evidently a matter of guess-work, which led to
curious irregularities in the elevation.   In this striking
instance, the builders were doubtless hampered by

having to build their new transept round older buildings, which were not taken down until their work was well advanced; and the encumbered site alone may account for some bewilderment.

§ 10.   Parish churches in England may be divided, for historical purposes, into four classes.   (1) In some monastic churches, as in the Benedictine priory of Selby and the Augustinian priory of Bridlington, the parochial altar was in the nave of the church, west of the rood screen, and was served by a vicar or a curate, who was responsible for the spiritual welfare of the parish.   (2) In collegiate churches a similar arrangement existed; but in the majority of such cases the dean or warden of the college was regarded as the parson of the parish, and had the cure of souls. (3) Of parish churches appropriated to monasteries, we have spoken already.   (4) There remains the very large number of unappropriated parish churches, in which the rector or parson was directly responsible for the cure of souls.   The duties of the rector were regarded in the middle ages with considerable latitude.   Nothing was more usual than for a man of good family, or one whose clerkly talents made him a constant attendant on the king or the great officers of state, to obtain a number of benefices which provided him with a necessary income.   Such parsons were naturally non-resident: as often as not, they had not proceeded to full orders.   The Patent Rolls

are full of grants of benefices to persons engaged in
the work of the royal chancery or exchequer ; while
the papal registers in the Vatican library contain
thousands of dispensations by which pluralists were
enabled to hold several benefices at a time, to acquire
benefices up to a stated value, or to defer their
ordination to the priesthood. Popes and bishops
alike kept a careful watch on the attempt to obtain
additional benefices without licence ; but it is quite
obvious that little discrimination could be exercised,
and that dispensations became matters of form, for
which the applicant, backed by a request from the
king or some magnate, made a payment in money.
Pluralism was further increased by the pope's claim
to reserve certain benefices on a vacancy, and provide
incumbents to them. This claim, which originally was
intended to prevent patrons from keeping benefices
vacant and appropriating their fruits, led to the
enactment of the statute of provisors in 1351. Papal
provisions, though nominally forbidden, were not
stopped by this law, but became subject to regulation.

§ 11. To the medieval mind, the habit of a non-
resident rector, holding several churches in plurality,
was a matter of course, which cannot be judged by
the moral standard of our own day. It must be
regarded simply as a fact, not as an abuse. The
rector was required to see that his churches were
properly served, and probably, like his successors

after the Reformation, he paid a curate to do his
work in each of his churches. In some cases, like
monastic impropriators, he made an arrangement by
which a vicar was provided with a fixed stipend ; and
now and then a vicar was properly instituted by the
bishop at his presentation. This was the regular
course of procedure in parish churches attached to
prebends in cathedral and collegiate churches, which
were held for the most part by king's clerks, and often
by foreigners appointed by the pope. But it is clear
that, where a man held ten or twelve churches at
once, they might be served very irregularly. Again,
no form of litigation in the middle ages was so common
as that between two or more claimants of an advowson.
The sub-division of the ownership of a manor might
and did constantly lead to a dispute between rival
patrons for the presentation to a living. Thus, in the
latter half of the thirteenth century, the church of
Adlingfleet in Yorkshire became the subject of a long
law-suit between two separate patrons, the archbishop
of York, and their presentees, which was protracted
for nearly thirty years before the royal and papal
courts. The candidates, all non-residents, strove to
obstruct each other. In the parish itself they made
attempts to defend their rights by force, and it is
difficult to see how, during this period of strife, the
cure of souls could have been adequately served.
Churches appropriated to monasteries were more

fortunate; for they, in most instances, had the advantage of a resident vicar, and the appropriation removed disputes as to the patronage.

§ 12. Pluralism and litigation, in themselves, had no noticeable effect on architectural development. But they led to a desire, on the part of the parishioners, for resident clergy with an endowment independent of the caprices of lay patrons. And this led to the establishment of chantry priests at the altars of churches, which had a powerful effect upon the architectural growth of the churches in which they served. Towards the end of the thirteenth century, and from that time to the Reformation, the foundation of chantries in parish churches became a common thing. Zeal for the foundation of monasteries had spent itself. Lay benefactors acquired the habit of alienating land, not to some religious house, but to one or more priests who, as a condition of the gift, should say mass daily at one of the altars of a parish church for the good estate of the giver and other persons named by him, and for their souls after death. These endowments of services were known as chantries, and were intended to continue for ever. Many chantries were founded in cathedral and monastery churches; but, as time went on, the church of the parish in which the benefactor lived was more and more frequently chosen as their site. That this had been always the custom is probable;

but it was a custom which certainly was not universal
until the later middle ages. From the time of the
enactment of the statute of mortmain, we possess a
series of royal licences for the foundation of chantries
and gifts of land to chantry priests, which are
invaluable in tracing the history of the English parish
church. A chantry, however, is a service, not the
building in which it is held. It might be founded
at the high altar of a church, but more usually was
connected with one of the lesser altars. It was
natural, however, that a founder would be willing to
do something for the repair of the part of the church
in which his chantry was held. Repair took the
form of enlargement and rebuilding; and while special
chantry chapels were sometimes built as excrescences
from the main body of the church, the usual building
which was done in connexion with a chantry implied
the widening or addition of an aisle.

§ 13. A good concrete example of this procedure
is the church of Beckingham, five miles east of
Newark-on-Trent, a building of various periods, but
chiefly of the early part of the thirteenth century.
The aisles of the nave are wide, and belong, in their
present condition, to the fourteenth century. At the
end of each are distinct indications of the former
presence of an altar. The parson of Beckingham in
the second quarter of the fourteenth century was
Thomas Sibthorpe, a man of some substance, and one

of the royal clerks. His benefactions to the church
of his native village of Sibthorpe and to Beckingham
involved him in some litigation, ample records of
which are to be found in the Patent Rolls. In 1332
he obtained a licence to found a chantry in the
chapel of St Mary, in the north part of Beckingham
church, and by the end of 1347, he built the chapel
of St Anne, on the south side of the church. Both
the existing chapels agree with one another in date ;
and we may safely infer that Sibthorpe probably
widened, and certainly rebuilt both the aisles between
1332 and 1347. He evidently intended his chapel of
St Mary to be of some importance, as the chantry
priest was called the warden, and was probably
intended to be the head of a small college, such as
existed at Sibthorpe. Of a chantry in the chapel of
St Anne we know nothing : Sibthorpe endowed two
candles to be burned there at certain times. An
interesting feature of this fourteenth century rebuilding is that the north and south doorways, both
of late twelfth century work, were removed to the
new walls.

§ 14. The growth of chantry foundations formed
the most remarkable feature of the lay activity of the
later middle ages, and is treated in the next chapter
with a view to its influence on architectural progress.
We may sum up the influence of the historical facts
already indicated upon the fabric of the parish church

in the following conclusions : (1) The origin of the parish church was the spiritual need of the private estate. (2) The lord of the manor was the founder and provided the fabric. (3) The work of the fabric was entrusted to local masons. (4) In the division of expense, the rector became responsible for the chancel and the altar from which he received his dues. (5) The parishioners were responsible for the fabric of the nave. (6) In churches appropriated to monasteries, the chancel was the only part of the fabric for which the monastery was responsible, and a part of its responsibility was usually laid upon the vicar. (7) Where the monastery was lord of the manor, it would take its share of the building and up-keep of the church with the other parishioners. We shall see in a later chapter some concrete instances of manorial and monastic influence at work upon the structure of the church.

CHAPTER II

§ 15. The chantry and the guild chapel had so important an influence on the plan of the parish church, and especially of the larger church, that they deserve further consideration, in company with the anomalies of plan which are their result. Chantries increased in number during the fourteenth century, and, from the period of the Black Death to the Reformation, had an ever growing importance. At Grantham, where it is clear that the enlargement of the church was due to the increase of chantries, three were founded in 1349, two of them at altars inside the church. In 1392 two new chantries were founded, at the altars of Holy Trinity and Corpus Christi, and the maintenance of chantries at the altars of St Mary and St John Baptist was increased by new benefactions. Thus, to large churches, a large staff of priests became attached. Although Grantham was never incorporated as a

collegiate church, the body of clergy which served it
seem to have had common services in quire together,
and to have been known as the ' college.'   The chantry
priests of a large church would benefit from incorporation in the ordinary course of things, and it very often
happened that they were formed into a regular college,
or that provisions were made affecting their common

Fig. 1.   Hallaton, Leicestershire : chapel in S. aisle.

life.   St William's college at York was founded for
the chantry priests of the minster in 1461 by archbishop Neville and his brother, the king-maker.   In
1482–3 archbishop Rotherham founded his college of
Jesus at Rotherham, to which, as a secondary provision
of the foundation, the chantry priests already existing
in the church were to be attached.   Rotherham

recognised that a large body of individual priests, whose
duties for the day were finished with their daily mass,
would be open to temptation if they were allowed to
choose their own lodgings as they liked ; and Thomas
Kent, whose executors in 1481 founded a 'perpetual
commonalty' of the seven chantry priests of St James
Garlickhithe in the city of London, expressed his
opinion that these chaplains 'conversed among laymen and wandered about, rather than dwelt among
clerks, as was decent.' Not infrequently, a benefactor
who wished to found a chantry of more than one
chaplain, acquired the advowson of the church in
which it was to be founded, and secured its appropriation to his chaplains, who held it in perpetuity,
and were incorporated as a college. This was the
case with the college of Sibthorpe. In 1333 Sir
John Heslerton, patron of the church of Lowthorpe
in east Yorkshire, founded a college of six priests
in the church, whose duties were set forth in detail
by archbishop Melton in his ordinance for the new
college, which included the appropriation of the
church to it. Sir John represented to the archbishop
that the fruits of the living would serve for the
maintenance of more than one parson, but that there
were few ministers there. 'Many persons there,' he
said, 'who are attached to the worship of the Holy
Trinity and St Mary, and are desirous of daily service
in their honour and for the departed, grow lukewarm

because of the frequent absence of anyone to celebrate
in the church, when their minister is engaged in the
visitation of the sick, or in discharge of the other
duties of his office.' Six chantries were founded, with
a priest to each, known as the chantries of the Trinity,
St Mary, the archbishop, the chapter, the founder,
and the patron. The head of the college was known
as the rector. He and the six chaplains had a
common habitation in the rectory. Daily they were
to assemble in the church, with the three clerks
attached to the college, one of whom at least was to
be a deacon, and chant the canonical services. The
chaplains were obliged to wear a common dress of
black or nearly dark cloth with black surcoats.

§ 16. The great advantage of colleges of chantry
priests was that they ensured a constantly resident
ministry in the parish. This, in days when rectors
were frequently non-residents or pluralists, whose
real business lay in attending on the king in the
chancery or exchequer, was a most desirable circumstance. But it is also quite easy to see that,
in a parish like Lowthorpe, a small country village
between Bridlington and Driffield, if there were too
few ministers before the foundation of the college,
there probably were too many after. Their duty, as
enunciated by the founder, was to celebrate divine
service for the departed; and this was a duty which,
sacred though it was, left those who were bound by

it a fair margin of leisure. Also, in some churches,
the chantry foundations were on a very large scale.
The college of Cotterstock in Northants was founded
in 1337 for a provost and twelve chaplains. In 1411
the college of Fotheringhay was founded, only two
miles away, for a master, twelve chaplains, eight
clerks, and thirteen choristers. Of the three chantry
colleges in Shropshire, Battlefield was founded at
first for a master and seven chaplains, to pray for
the dead who fell at the battle of Shrewsbury; Tong
was founded in 1410 for a warden and four chaplains;
Newport was enlarged from a chantry of two chaplains, founded in 1432, to a college of a warden and
four chaplains in 1442. Other colleges which may be
cited out of many were Haccombe in Devon, founded
in 1335 for an arch-priest and five chaplains; Bunbury
in Cheshire, founded in 1386–7 for a master and six
chaplains; Clovelly in Devon, founded in 1387–8 for
a warden and six chaplains; Pleshy in Essex, founded
in 1393–4 for a master or warden, eight chaplains,
two clerks, and two choristers; Higham Ferrers in
Northants, founded in 1425 for a master or warden,
seven chaplains, four clerks, and six choristers;
Tattershall in Lincolnshire, founded in 1439 for a
master or warden, six chaplains, six secular clerks,
and six choristers, with thirteen almspeople; and
Middleham in Yorkshire, founded in 1477–8 for a
dean, six chaplains, four clerks, six choristers, and one

secular clerk. All these foundations bore a distinct
resemblance to the ordinary collegiate bodies, such as
those of the cathedrals, or of Wolverhampton, Tamworth, Bridgnorth, or Westbury-on-Trym. But, while
the holders of prebends in collegiate churches were
not necessarily, and indeed were seldom, resident, the
fellows or chaplains of chantry colleges were obliged
to be always on the spot. Nor were these chantries
of more than one priest founded merely in parish
churches. Lords of manors founded chantries on
their estates : there was a college of several chantry
priests at the Beauchamp castle of Elmley in Worcestershire, for example. Sir Robert Umfraville,
who founded in 1429 a chantry of a master and
a chaplain in the chapel of his manor house at
Farnacres, near Gateshead, strictly bound down the
incumbents to their religious duties, forbidding them
to carry on any temporal business as bailiffs or estate
agents, on the ground that *dum colitur Martha,
expellitur Maria.*

§ 17. The foundation of ordinary chantries more
than kept pace with the foundation of chantry
colleges. Individual benefactors sought to secure
their own salvation and that of their relations, by
endowing an altar in their parish church. In parishes
where services were few, the parishioners often club-
bed together for the support of a stipendiary service,
paid out of property of which they were feoffees.

The chaplain whose services were thus secured would be of great use to the incumbent of a large parish, especially at seasons when there were many communicants, and many confessions had to be heard. Also, in distant parts of large parishes, separated from the mother church by several miles, or by foul roads and flooded streams in winter, chantry priests were provided by individual or collective benefactions to serve the altars of parochial chapels. In the great parishes of west Yorkshire, Burnsall, Aysgarth, or Grinton, each including a vast tract of dale and fell, parochial chapels, subject to the mother church, had existed from a very early period. Such chapels became more numerous as the middle ages advanced; and the famous chapel of South Skirlaugh, between Hull and Hornsea, so often quoted as a perfect example of late Gothic work, was one of these subordinate foundations. It may also be noted that two of the largest parish churches of the same neighbourhood, St Augustine's at Hedon and Holy Trinity at Hull, were originally chapels to Preston-in-Holderness and Hessle. At Boughton in Northants, owing to a shifting of the population, a chapel in the parish became the parish church. Obviously, if the larger churches were to be properly served, they must depend in no small measure on the goodwill of the parishioners.

§ 18.   In the fourteenth and fifteenth centuries

the parishioners came forward with benefactions as they never had done before. The rich wool stapler of Grantham, Newark, or Boston, returned thanks for his wealth by founding a chantry in his church or one of its chapels. With the rise of the commercial class, the churches of East Anglia were rebuilt and transformed. Wealthy trade guilds at York, Boston, Shrewsbury, or Coventry, maintained their own chaplains in the various parish churches. Religious guilds or fraternities, composed both of men and women, obtained royal licence for incorporation, and established their chantries. Such was the Palmers' guild at Ludlow, which received its first royal charter in 1284, and maintained a large body of chantry priests, incorporated as a college, in the parish church. These religious guilds existed for the purpose of mutual assistance and works of charity. The guilds of St Mary and Corpus Christi in Cambridge united together in one corporation, and founded Corpus Christi college in 1352. In 1392 the guild of St Mary at Stamford had licence to devote land to the maintenance of certain chantry priests in St Mary's at the Bridge. In the same year, two guilds at Coventry were united under the name of the guild of the Holy Trinity, St Mary, and St John the Baptist, and founded a college of chaplains in St John's chapel at Bablake. Still in 1392, the guild of the Holy Cross at Birmingham was founded, with its chaplains in St Martin's; and the

guilds of St Mary and of Jesus Christ and the Holy
Cross in the parish church of Chesterfield. To 1393
belongs the foundation of the guild of the Holy
Trinity at Spalding, with a chaplain at the Trinity
altar in the parish church. In the reign of Henry
IV the refounded guild of St Cross and St John the
Baptist at Stratford-on-Avon had licence to find two
or more chaplains in their parish church (1403);
the guild of St Thomas of Canterbury, with one
or two chaplains, was founded at Long Sutton in
Lincolnshire (1405). Under Henry VI may be mentioned the guild of St Mary at Louth, with more
than one chaplain, founded in 1446–7; the licence
to the guild of the Holy Trinity at Nottingham, in
the same year, to maintain two chaplains in St Mary's
church; the guild of St Mary of Crediton, with a
chaplain at the altar of St Peter, founded in 1448;
the guilds of the Holy Trinity, with two chaplains,
at Chipping Norton, and, with one or more chaplains,
at Louth (1450); and the guild of St Mary, with two
chaplains, at Chipping Sodbury in Gloucestershire
(1452). In 1460–1, the twelve chaplains, supported
by seven guilds, in All Saints, Northampton, were
formed into a college. In the time of Edward IV
the trade guilds became more active in establishing
chantries; but the foundation of religious guilds went
on with unabated zeal. A number were founded in the
small market-towns of Bedfordshire, Buckinghamshire,

and Hertfordshire, with aid in more than one instance from the diocesan, Thomas Rotherham, then bishop of Lincoln—the fraternity of the Body of Jesus Christ at Leighton Buzzard (1473), the guilds of the Holy Trinity at Luton (1474) and Biggleswade (1474–5), a guild at Hitchin (1475), and the guild of St Mary and St Thomas the Martyr at Stony Stratford (1476). In 1480 was founded a guild at Thaxted in Essex, and in 1483–4 the fraternity of the Holy Cross at Abingdon.

§ 19. The names of most of these guilds, which were joined by royal and noble personages, are connected with churches of great beauty and importance, which owe their final perfection in no small degree to the benefactions of the brethren and sisters of the guilds. The chapel of Bablake, St John Baptist's church at Coventry, was a result of the incorporation of the guilds in 1392. The two guilds at Louth and Chesterfield left their mark on the churches in which they worshipped. The chancel, the aisles of the nave, the great porches, the west tower and spire, at Thaxted, belong to the epoch, if they are not altogether the direct result, of the foundation of the guild. Chantry chapels and guild chapels may exert their influence on the plan of the fabric, simply by providing it with a complete set of aisles. Of this type of plan, we already have seen an example at Beckingham. But these chapels often cause anomalies which are difficult to

classify, and lead to some confusion of plan; and
some instances of this character must now be given.
In the first place, the chantry chapel is not confined
to any definite part of the plan.   In our cathedrals it
is frequently an excrescence from an outer wall of the
church, like the bishops' tomb chapels at Lincoln or
Hereford, or it is a rectangular structure of stone, with
elaborately traceried windows, cresting, and canopy
work, like prince Arthur's chapel at Worcester, or the
episcopal tombs at Winchester, set up within an arch of
the nave or quire.   Of these types we have examples
in our parish churches: the first is illustrated, on a
large scale, by Hall's chapel at Grantham; on a fair
scale, by the chapels at Long Melford and Berkeley;
and, on a rather smaller scale, by the chapels, now
destroyed, of two masters of Peterhouse, on either
side of Little St Mary's church at Cambridge.   All
these have small doorways and arches for table
tombs between the church and the chapel.   The
chapel east of the south porch at Sherburn-in-Elmet
in Yorkshire, has a tomb arch opening into the south
aisle; but the entrance is in the east wall of the porch.
Many examples of the second type must have existed
in the larger churches of England: at Ludlow, for
example, there were chantry chapels in the eastern
arch of the south arcade, and in the two western
arches of both arcades.   We read of Sir John
Pilkington's chantry, founded in 1475 at the altar of

St Mary in the 'south arch' of the parish church
at Wakefield: in 1478 the chantry of Roger Nowell
was founded at the altar of St Peter in the
'north arch.'   There are stone chantry chapels
in the north and south arches of the chancel
at Newark—the chantry chapel of Thomas Meyring
(1500) on the north, and that of Robert Markham
(1505) on the south.   These chapels recall prior
Byrde's chapel at Bath abbey, the Warre chapel at
Boxgrove priory, and other small independent structures, like some of the tomb chapels which form a ring
round the apse at Tewkesbury.   Most of these chapels
beneath arches were no doubt covered, like prior
Leishman's tomb at Hexham, with wooden canopies,
which have now disappeared.   At Burford in Oxfordshire, however, there is, in the east arch of the north
arcade, a small chapel with a wooden tester and
upright posts: the sides are panelled up to a certain
height.   The whole structure has been well restored
and is still used.

§ 20.   Some small chantry chapels form transeptal
projections in unusual parts of the building: thus, at
Sherburn-in-Elmet, St Botolph's, Cambridge, and
Kewstoke, Somerset, such chapels project from the
south wall of the nave next the porch.   Indeed, the
variety in the position of chantry chapels often invests
the churches of the west of England with a charm
which is not always possessed by more regular

buildings. Churches like Beverstone in Gloucestershire, Croscombe in Somerset, and Sherston Magna
in Wiltshire, are full of little surprises for anyone to
whom variations in plan appeal. Perhaps the most
attractive surprise of this kind is at Long Melford in
Suffolk. On the south side of the chancel, opening
out of the Martin chapel, is a vestry, which com-
municates with another building at right angles to
it, behind the east wall of the chancel. From this
building there is a doorway into the lady chapel,
which thus stands detached from the body of the
church. The chapel is a nearly square building, with
three external gables: internally, there is a central
square space, entirely surrounded by an aisle or
ambulatory. At Boston there is a chantry chapel,
forming a short extra aisle, west of the south porch;
while at Witney, there is one west of the north porch.
Sometimes, the whole of an aisle of the nave, east of
the main entrance of the church, was screened off as a
chantry chapel. There are instances of this at Croft
in Yorkshire, Hungerton in Leicestershire, and
Stratton Strawless in Norfolk. There are instances,
again, in which, when a chantry chapel was placed at
the end of an aisle, its separate character from the
rest of the aisle was structurally defined. In Shropshire, at Alveley, Cleobury Mortimer, Stottesdon, and
one or two other places, one or more chantry chapels
have been formed by widening the eastern part of the
aisles in which the altars were placed.

§ 21. Where chantry colleges have existed, the fact is by no means always obvious in the plan of the church. It is sometimes disclosed by the presence of stall-work of unusual richness in the chancel, as at Higham Ferrers; and sometimes, as in the same place, the altar in the main chancel may have been reserved for the services of the college, while another altar was provided for the ordinary parochial services. But it must be borne in mind that a chantry college was not a monastery. The church appropriated to the college was a parish church. Although a chaplain might be specially deputed to look after parochial services, the master, rector, warden, provost, arch-priest, or whatever his title might be, was in the position of a resident incumbent. Many splendid churches, now shorn of their chancels, recall the fact that the naves of monastic churches were frequently used for the services of the parish. This distinction doubtless extended to many chantry colleges, Arundel and Fotheringhay, for example. But the services of the college were not cut off, like the services of the monastery, from the outer world. The college of Lowthorpe was founded specifically for the benefit of devout parishioners who, before its foundation, could not get all the masses they wanted. The result is that the plan of the chantry church, as it may be called, differed little from that of the ordinary parish church. Sibthorpe and Cotterstock

are normal churches, with fine chancels: the altars at
which each of the three chaplains of Chaddesden, or
the four of St Michael Penkivel, said his daily mass,
are not confined to one part of the church, but are
distributed throughout it. Colleges at Oxford and
Cambridge, which were originally colleges of clergy,
were practically identical with chantry colleges, with
the exception that their members were associated
mainly for purposes of study and teaching. To many
of them parish churches were appropriated, in which
they held their services, and maintained their own
parochial chaplain. St Michael's at Cambridge, appropriated to Michaelhouse, was rebuilt in the early
part of the fourteenth century. It has been little
altered, and the division into collegiate quire and
parochial nave is clearly marked. There was a similar
division in Little St Mary's, belonging to Peterhouse.
In the fourteenth century the college began to rebuild
the church on a large scale. The chancel was nearly completed, when the Black Death put a stop to the work.
Later, an extra western bay was added to the chancel;
and the aisleless church thus formed was divided by a
screen into a collegiate and a parochial half. In 1446
Clare hall and Trinity hall added aisles to the chancel
of St Edward's: these aisles were wider than the aisles
of the nave, and also overlapped the nave by one bay.
When Jesus college entered into possession of the
nunnery of St Radegund, the priory church was shorn

of the western end of the nave and of all its aisles.
The college reserved the quire for its own services,
while the parishioners of the old peculiar of the
priory used the nave and transepts. The ante-chapel
of Merton college chapel at Oxford was used till
quite lately as the parish church of St John Baptist.

§ 22. No better instance of the complicating
influence of chantry chapels on the plan of a parish
church could be given than the church of St John
Baptist at Cirencester. The oldest part of the present
building is the chancel with its south chapel, which
contain twelfth and early thirteenth century work, but
are in the main the fruit of a later thirteenth century
reconstruction. The north chapel, known as St
Katharine's chapel, is a rather narrow aisle, com-
municating with the chancel by fourteenth century
arches. North of this, again, there may have been a
lady chapel on part of the site of the present one.
Towards the middle of the fifteenth century, the aisles
of the nave were much widened, the width taken for
the new north aisle being about twice the width of
St Katharine's chapel, and the new south aisle being
rather wider than the south chapel of the chancel.
The Trinity chapel was formed by adding to the nave an
extra north aisle, about half as long as the adjacent
aisle, from which it is divided by a stone screen. There
had been an earlier altar of the Trinity in the church;
for the licence granted to Robert Playn and others in

1382 to found a chantry of two chaplains in Cirencester
church placed one at the altar of the Trinity, and the
other at the altar of St Mary. In 1392 another

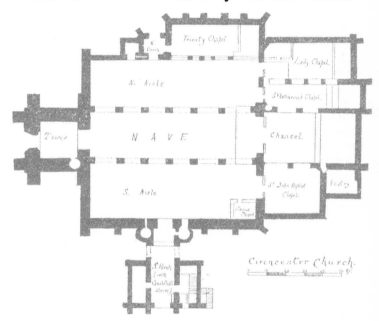

Fig. 2. Plan of Cirencester Church.

chantry was founded in the lady chapel. But, in its
present state, the lady chapel seems to belong to the

later part of the fifteenth century, when it was probably much broadened, so as to overlap the east wall of
the Trinity chapel. Both it and St Katharine's chapel
open into the north aisle through four-centred arches:
they open into one another by two arches pierced
in the intermediate wall. Between these arches has
been left a thin piece of wall, in which rectangular
slits, commanding the altar of the lady chapel, have
been cut. The plan thus includes two chapels north
of the chancel, and another north of the nave, as well
as the south chapel of the chancel. The rebuilding
of the nave, with its splendid south porch, its smaller
north porch, and its western tower, was not completed
until early in the sixteenth century. The Jesus chapel
was enclosed within screens at the south-east corner
of the south aisle; and the roof of St Katharine's
chapel was heightened, and provided with fan vaulting.

§ 23. The tendency of the chantry chapels at
Cirencester is to group themselves at the east end of
the church, the Trinity chapel forming an excrescence
at the end of the north aisle which is nearest the
chancel. At Chesterfield the high altar, below the
great east window, was flanked by the guild chapel
of our Lady on the south, and the chapel of St
Katharine on the north. The guild chapel of the
Holy Cross was east of the north transept: an apsidal
chapel east of the south transept contained the altar
of St George; while there were two chantry altars

against the screens in the arches of the south transept. The four chantry chapels added to Scarborough church towards the end of the fourteenth century were built in a row at right angles to the south aisle, each with its own separate gable and pointed barrel vault. The chapel of St Nicholas had been added to the church somewhat earlier, by the building of an extra north aisle; a chantry was founded at St Nicholas' altar in 1390. We also meet at Scarborough, Great Yarmouth, and other places, with charnel chapels. That at Scarborough, dedicated to St Mary Magdalene, was probably a separate building in the graveyard. Such external chapels were often built, although few remain to-day. Henry of Newark, archbishop of York 1298–9, founded about 1292, while he was dean of York, a chapel of St Katharine and St Martha in the churchyard of Newark. Some twenty years later, when the enlargement of the aisles of Newark church was contemplated, archbishop Grenefeld licensed the destruction of the chapel. Its materials were used for the rebuilding of the south aisle, and the chantry was probably transferred to an altar in the new building. There was probably a charnel chapel at Grantham, to the south-west of the church.

§ 24. But the most interesting case of an external chapel is the Sylvester chapel at Burford, which now forms a long arm stretching to the south-west of the

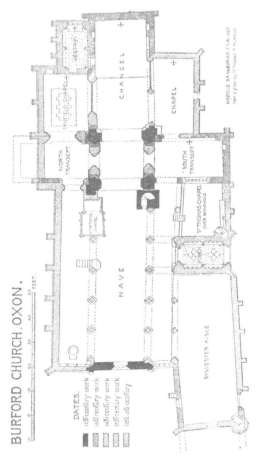

BURFORD CHURCH. OXON.

DATES.
- 12th century work
- 13th century work
- 14th century work
- 15th century work
- 16th & 17th century

VESTRY

TANFIELD CHAPEL

CHANCEL

CHAPEL

NORTH TRANSEPT

SOUTH TRANSEPT

ST PETER'S CHAPEL

NAVE

ST THOMAS CHAPEL (OVER BONEHOLE)

PORCH

SYLVESTER AISLE

HAROLD BRAKSPEAR F.S.A. del.

Now open by H. Thomas W. Plaistow

Fig. 3. Plan of Burford Church.

main fabric. The church and chapel were originally
separate. The church was, to begin with, an aisleless
twelfth century structure, with a tower between nave
and chancel. In the thirteenth century the chancel
was produced to its present length, the north and
south walls of the tower were pierced with arches,
and transeptal chapels were added. A narrow south
aisle was also added to the nave. About the same
time a long aisleless chapel was built in the churchyard, some yards to the south-west of the church. In
the fourteenth century a chapel was constructed, with
a bone-crypt beneath it, west of the south transept,
and was connected with the south aisle. There seems
to have been no north aisle to the nave. East of the
transepts were small chapels. The fifteenth century
saw a great transformation. A sacristy was built
north of the altar. Aisles and a south porch of great
beauty were built in harmony with a new nave arcade.
The outer chapel, the axis of which was not parallel
to that of the nave, was prolonged eastward to meet
the south porch, and connected by an arcade with the
south aisle. It was shortened at the west end, but
still projects two bays beyond the main body of the
church. The east chapel of the south transept was
now taken away, and a south chancel chapel built,
the east wall of which interfered with the thirteenth
century sedilia of the chancel. The south wall of the
chancel, opposite the sacristy, was allowed to stand

clear of the new chapel. On the opposite side of the church, the north transept was shortened, until it was little longer than the breadth of the north aisle : its north wall was then continued eastwards and was returned to join the west wall of the sacristy. The north chapel of the chancel was thus formed. The whole progress of the plan is from a simple form of aisleless church to an aisled rectangle with central tower and spire ; but the process is irregular, and the absorption of the outer chapel is an almost unique step. It will be noticed that the south aisle is entirely covered by a triple arrangement of buildings—first, St Thomas' chapel next the south transept, then the south porch, and finally the Sylvester chapel, which gives additional length to the church from this point of view.

§ 25. Other examples of churches in the wealthy market towns of the west of England might be given, in which, as at Frome, chantry chapels grafted themselves upon the plan, with immense advantage to the picturesque effect. But there were few churches on which the foundation of chantries, and especially of chantries maintained by religious guilds, had such influence as on the great churches of Coventry— St Michael's, Holy Trinity, and St John's. Licences for the foundations of chantries in St Michael's bear date 1323 (two chaplains), 1344 (one chaplain in the chapel of St Lawrence, augmented 1383, 1390), 1388

(one chaplain at the altar of All Saints), 1411–2 (one
chaplain at the altar of St Katharine), and 1412
(two chaplains at the newly made altars of the Holy
Trinity and St Mary).   In addition to these altars and
the high altar there were altars of Jesus, St John,
St Anne, St Thomas, and St Andrew.   The chantries
at these various altars became in time attached to the

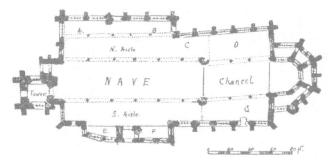

Fig. 4.   Plan of St Michael's, Coventry.   A. St Andrew's Chapel.
   B. Girdlers' Chapel.   C. St Lawrence's Chapel.   D. Drapers'
   Chapel.   E. Dyers' Chapel.   F. Cappers' Chapel.   G. Mercers'
   Chapel.

various trade guilds of the town, and the church,
greatly enlarged and extended in the fifteenth and
early sixteenth centuries, contained several chapels,
known by the names of the guilds.   Some details of
the rebuilding have been touched upon already.   The
plan is curious; for the chancel ends in a semi-

octagonal apse—a feature which also occurs in the late Gothic chancels of Westbury-on-Trym and Wrexham—surrounded by a row of vestries on a lower level. On the north of the chancel is the lady chapel, the altar of which was new in 1412–3, known later as the drapers' chapel. The south chapel of the chancel was the mercers' chapel, which probably contained the Trinity altar. The eastern part of the north aisle

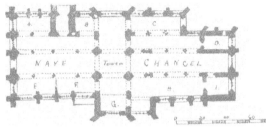

Fig. 5. Plan of Holy Trinity Church, Coventry. A. Archdeacon's Court. B. St Thomas' Chapel. C. Marler's Chapel. D. Lady Chapel. E. Tanners' Chapel. F. Jesus Chapel. G. Corpus Christi Chapel. H. Butchers' Chapel. I. Holy Trinity Chapel.

was occupied by St Lawrence's chapel. The outer north aisle was divided into two parts : east of the doorway was All Saints' or the girdlers' chapel, while west of it was St Andrew's or the smiths' chapel. Two further chapels, St Thomas' or the cappers' chapel, and the dyers' chapel, formed excrescences to east and west of the south porch. The beautiful

cruciform church of the Holy Trinity became flanked
in process of time by similar chapels. In the later
part of the thirteenth century the north porch was
joined to the transept by St Thomas' chapel. At a
later date a chapel, afterwards the consistory court,
was built from the west wall of the north porch as far
as the west wall of the north aisle. Much later, in
the sixteenth century, Marler's or the mercers' chapel
was continued from the east wall of the north transept along the north aisle of the quire, the north
transept being thus practically absorbed in an outer
north aisle. The lady chapel was at the end of the
north aisle of the chancel, north of the altar : opposite
it, on the south, was the Trinity chapel. The south
aisle of the chancel was the butchers' chapel : in the
south transept was the Corpus Christi chapel, now
destroyed ; while at the west end of the south aisle of
the nave was the tanners' chapel.

§ 26. Thus, by the gradual addition of chapel
after chapel, the plan of these magnificent churches,
some of the finest productions of English art, grew
until, as at Burford or Holy Trinity, Coventry, it lost
all likeness to its original state, and seems at first
sight to be a collection of buildings heaped together
without much method. It would be interesting to
trace the growth of churches like St Mary Redcliffe
or Ludlow, as we have traced that of Cirencester and
Burford. In these cases, it is impossible to give too

much emphasis to the part played by lay benefactors
in the development of the fabric. Cirencester, Burford, and the Coventry churches, were appropriated
to monasteries: St Mary Redcliffe was merely a
chapel of Bedminster, appropriated, like Grantham,
to a stall in Salisbury cathedral. At Cirencester and
Coventry the churches were close to the religious
houses to which they belonged. But the growth of
the churches was the result of lay devotion: the
founders of chantries of whom we hear, like the
famous William Canynge at St Mary Redcliffe, were
men who had made money in business. The part of
the monasteries in church-building was never, so far
as parish churches were concerned, very active. As
the middle ages went on, their connexion with the
fabrics became still slighter; and their interest in
the church, apart from the profits which they received
from it, and from an occasional litigation about the
advowson, was probably confined to the periodical
presentation of a vicar. The highest state of development which the parish church attained, in such
buildings as have just been described, or in the great
churches of Norfolk and Somerset, was the consequence
of a long series of beautifications and improvements,
in which at first, no doubt, the lay lords of manors
took the leading part, but afterwards were joined by
wealthy parishioners, who could find no more fitting
employment for their wealth than the enlargement

and decoration of the house of God. And it should
not be forgotten that not merely the rich, but the
poor, shared in this work of benefaction. In some
places, at Oswestry, for example, chantry priests were
supported by the devotion of servants or husbandmen,
each of whom paid his yearly share of the endowment.
Here and there in East Anglia, inscriptions remaining
on beautiful pieces of church furniture, bear witness
to the generosity of members of the parish in humble
positions. The churches of London, Bristol, York,
and Norwich, and of countless towns and villages, are
memorials of the brightest aspect of medieval religion
—the spontaneous devotion which it excited, for
motives often mingled with superstition, but never
selfish or unworthy, in the most hard-headed and
least emotional section, then as now, of English society.

CHAPTER III

THE TOWER, THE PORCH, AND THE CHANCEL

§ 27. In another volume of this series, the development of the ground plan of the parish church has been treated with some detail. The importance of the central tower in connexion with the transeptal or cruciform plan has there been explained; and it has been seen that English builders generally preferred a tower at the west end of the nave. In the present chapter, something will be said of the development and use of the western tower, and of the closely related subject of the entrances to the church. The nave and its aisles demand, in this space, little more attention than can be given to them in the discussion of the ground plan and in what has been said already with regard to chantry chapels; and of their furniture more will be said in the next chapter. But some further consideration of the chancel, the enlargement of which forms so important a part of the history of the medieval plan, is necessary; and some account of its architectural and ritual development is given here, following the description of the tower and porch.

Fig. 6. Norton, Co. Durham: Saxon central tower, with transept.

§ 28. There is evidence that, in certain churches of unquestionably Saxon origin, the western tower was formed, probably at a time considerably subsequent to their foundation, by the heightening of the western porch or main entrance to the church. Brixworth and Monkwearmouth are cases in point. At Brixworth the original western doorway of the porch was blocked up when the stair-turret of the tower was built on that side. At Monkwearmouth the line of the gabled roof of the porch is still visible. Western towers, whether heightened or built from the ground, were certainly not common until, at any rate, the epoch of the Danish wars. No existing church can be assigned positively to that epoch; and those who contend that the church tower then came into existence as a place of defence and refuge from the invaders probably argue from analogies of a later period. The thin walls and undefended ground-floor doorways of Saxon towers forbid us to entertain this theory seriously. But it is certainly the case that these towers, primarily intended as bell-towers, were sometimes planned to afford more accommodation than was necessary for a man whose sole duty was to ring the bell. The ground-floor area of towers like Earl's Barton and Barnack in Northants, and Hough-on-the-Hill in Lincolnshire, which, in their present state, may be assigned tentatively to the later part of the tenth century, takes its place in the history of the development of the plan; and, just as at Barton-on-Humber, the dimensions of the upper part of such towers were conditioned by the space allotted to the lowest stage. But there are indications that, in cases where the ground floor of the tower was simply the porch of the church, one or more of the upper stages had their special use. A doorway occasionally has been made in the east wall of the tower, above the arch leading into the nave. This may be explained by the fact that such towers were small in area, and that their angles contained no room for staircases. Some access from the interior of the church to their upper stories was necessary, and would be easily provided by a ladder from the ground floor to the doorway on the first floor. The doorway is usually slightly on one side of the centre of the wall, so that the ladder would not interfere with the archway below. But the case is different, when, as at Brixworth, a large circular turret has been built against the west wall of the tower, and from the first floor chamber there is a large triple window-opening looking out into the body of the church. At Deerhurst, there is not only a doorway in the first floor of the tower; but, close by it, near the centre of the wall, there is a small window-opening or squint; while, on the second floor, there is a double window-opening of unusual form, and, on the third floor, another doorway in the centre of the wall, which seems to have opened into a wooden gallery. More than this, the lower part of the tower is partitioned by a transverse wall into an eastern and western porch and upper chamber. It is therefore indisputable that the tower at Deerhurst was more than a bell-tower. Deerhurst was an important monastery: the size and plan of the church were exceptional; and the upper floors of the tower may have been used for special purposes in connexion with the monastic services. One may hazard the suggestion that the room on the east side of the first floor was used by the monk whose turn it was to keep night-watch in the church: the spy-hole in the east wall seems to afford ground for this. It has been suggested that the second floor chamber—and, like it, the first floor chamber at Brixworth—was used as an oratory by the lord of the manor and protector of the monastery; and this is possible, if the importance of the lord of the manor in connexion with early parish churches is taken into account. Almery-like recesses in the wall are found in this chamber at Deerhurst: such recesses, where they are found by themselves, as in the tower of Skipwith in Yorkshire, suggest little and prove nothing, and at Deerhurst no positive reason for their use can be given. In some medieval churches there are traces of altars on the upper floors of towers; and it is possible that such altars may have existed at Deerhurst and Brixworth, and the windows pierced in the wall

behind them may have been given special decorative
treatment. The western stair-turret at Brixworth
was probably constructed for the sake of the important first floor chamber. Three other examples
of a circular stair-turret projecting from the western
face of a tower are found, one in Northamptonshire,
two in Lincolnshire ; but in none of these are there
any indications of a particular use for the first floor
of the tower. The only example of a spiral stair or
vice built in an angle of a pre-Conquest tower is
at Great Hale in Lincolnshire, and is a rude piece of
work. Until the introduction of buttresses, the
newel stair in the angle of the tower was uncommon.
A ladder from the floor of the tower served for access
to the upper stages. In rare instances, as at Kirkburn in the east riding of Yorkshire, a stone stair
was built against the inner walls of the tower as far
as the level of the first floor. Where angle-staircases
have been added to early Norman towers, as at
Tansor in Northants or in the central tower at Coln
St Denis in Gloucestershire, the abutments have
been seriously weakened.

§ 29. In the eleventh century, the western bell-
tower, the ground floor of which served as the main
porch of the church, became common. The tower of
the so-called 'Lincolnshire' type, with its stages
separated by off-sets, and its double belfry window
openings divided by a 'mid-wall' shaft, is found not

Fig. 7. Carlton-in-Lindrick, Notts.: west tower, of late Saxon type, with later additions.

infrequently in other parts of England, and survived, with some change in proportion and detail, for some time after the Norman Conquest. Some sixty western towers of the ordinary late Saxon type remain in England, exclusive of heightened porches, and of a few round towers in the eastern counties, where the absence of stone suitable for quoins made this shape desirable. It is probable that portions of many more exist beneath later additions. We have seen that in the tower at Branston, built more than a quarter of a century at earliest after the Conquest, the old type was retained—the slender tower, lofty in proportion to its area. The tower of Weaverthorpe in the east riding of Yorkshire, obviously Norman in its details, keeps the old proportions. Many towers, on the contrary, which, at first sight, might be associated with the Saxon group, shew Norman influence in the thickness of their walls and stoutness of their proportions. While the normal thickness of wall in the late Saxon towers of Lincolnshire is about three and a half feet, the thickness at Caistor is increased to nearly six feet. The normal area is from ten to twelve feet square : the area at Caistor is $15\frac{1}{2}$ feet east to west by $17\frac{1}{2}$ north to south. The normal width of the arch between tower and nave is about $5\frac{3}{4}$ feet : at Caistor it is nearly four feet more. At Tugby, between Leicester and Uppingham, there is a remarkable tower, built in a primitive fashion which shews distinct traces of Saxon kinship, but with proportions and with the introduction of detail which as clearly bear witness to its post-Conquest date. Hooton Pagnell, near Doncaster, has a large western tower which follows the Saxon tradition of the simple rubble tower with small stone quoins and without buttresses ; but the character of the arch leading into the nave is distinctly Norman, and the tower is not merely of unusually large area, but is the full breadth of the spacious nave beyond it. While the western tower increases in area, it does not at first acquire buttresses at the angles : these, in their flat pilaster-like form, begin to appear in the course of the twelfth century.

§ 30. The magnificent architectural development of the tower and spire, in which, as in perhaps no other part of the church, the individual characteristics of local schools of masoncraft can be traced, becomes noticeable in the thirteenth century, at a time when the use of the ground floor of the tower as the principal porch of the church had been discontinued. In the fen country round Wisbech and Spalding, a series of thirteenth century towers, covering the period from 1200 to 1280, bears witness to the work of a school of tower builders, hardly less distinguished than the great Somerset masons of later days, which probably derived its inspiration from the arcaded western tower of Ely cathedral. Elm, Leverington,

Walsoken, West Walton, Tilney All Saints, Long
Sutton, Gedney, and Whaplode, are the principal
evidence of their work. Not all these towers are
western, and four of the number, including Gedney,
the belfry stage of which belongs to a later date, are
without the spires which their builders doubtless
intended; but all are instances of the treatment of
the bell-tower as an independent architectural composition, quite irrespective of its part in the plan
of the church. In the twelfth century, however,
when the side doorway was superseding the tower
porch, the western tower was by no means so handsome or invariable a feature as it became in later
days. Many smaller churches were content with a
bell-cot over the western gable. There are several
excellent examples of stone bell-cots in Rutland. In
Essex and other districts where good building timber
was easily procured, it is not uncommon to find
square towers of timber, with conical caps or even
spires, above the western gable, often supported on
an elaborate framework within the west end of the
church. A few timber towers, like Margaretting in
Essex, are built up against the old west end of the
church.

§ 31. There can be no doubt that, in the earlier
part of the middle ages, while the high pitched roof
prevailed in the main body of the building, the spire
was considered the proper termination of a tower.

Its chief development naturally took place in districts
where good roofing stone was plentiful; and the finest
English spires, with a few exceptions, are to be found
in south Lincolnshire, Northamptonshire, Leicestershire, and Rutland. In less favoured districts, timber
spires, covered with lead or shingles, were placed upon
towers. Many of these remain in Surrey and Sussex.
The spire may be regarded as the natural development
of the conical roofs with which the towers of the
eleventh and early twelfth centuries were usually
crowned—an invaluable, if exceptional, example of
which remains at Sompting, near Worthing. These
must generally have been of wood with leaden
coverings. The earliest general development of the
stone spire is probably to be traced to south Lincolnshire, where the low broach spires of Sleaford,
Rauceby, Frampton, and a few other churches,
appear to belong to the last years of the twelfth,
or earliest years of the thirteenth century. The
spire continued to be fashionable in this and the
neighbouring districts, long after it had become
unusual in other parts of England. Grantham spire
exercised an enduring influence upon its neighbourhood. It was the model upon which the builders of
the spire of Oakham endeavoured to improve, with
less striving after height and more coherence of
design. From Oakham was closely derived the tower
of Exton in Rutland, where the builders raised their

spire upon an octagonal base. The octagon at Exton
was probably the parent of those octagons which,
rising on the summit of towers, reach their climax in
the lantern at Boston, and in the octagonal frame
which surrounds the lower part of the spire at
Patrington. Other details at Exton bore fruit in the
spires of Oundle and Kettering. At the very end of
the middle ages, the feeling for the spire in Lincolnshire was still so strong that the tower of Louth was
designed for a spire in the middle of the fifteenth
century, and the spire itself was brought to completion
in 1515.

§ 32. While, in the districts to which allusion
has just been made, towers were designed, as a rule,
with a view to the spires which were to cover them,
the tower, in other parts of England, was designed
simply as a tower, and the spire was regarded merely
as a roof for it. In the chalk country north of the
Thames, towers are often found crowned by small
timber spirelets with a leaden covering, which are
merely insignificant additions. Towards the middle
of the fourteenth century, an important development
in the elevation of the main fabric led to a general
disuse of the spire, especially in districts where stone
spires had formed no part of architectural design.
Clerestories with broad windows were built above
the arcades of the nave. With this increase of
height the old high pitched roofs were abandoned

Fig. 8. Tickhill, Yorkshire: general view from S.E., showing clerestory, western tower and projecting eastern chapel.

in favour of roofs of a flatter pitch. Very often, this
was due to the rotting of the old roof-timber at the
ends next the wall-plates. These ends were sawn
off, and the roof re-laid at a lower pitch. At the
same time, the clerestory dwarfed the western tower.
At Oadby, near Leicester, where there is a beautiful
tower and spire, designed in perfect harmony with
a fourteenth century nave, the fifteenth century
clerestory actually raises the height of the nave to
that of the tower, with incongruous effect. During
the fifteenth century, therefore, it is common to find
that towers were rebuilt, or an upper story was added
to them, in proportion to the increase of height in
the nave. Thus, at Immingham in north Lincolnshire, the clerestory and upper part of the tower are
of one date, and were built as part of one connected
work. The roof of the clerestory being, in most
cases, nearly flat, the roof of the tower followed suit;
and although, where traditions of spire design had a
hardy existence, spires were still built, towers without
spires, surmounted by parapets like the parapets
which hid the roof of the clerestories, became the
order of the day. In certain parts of England, and
especially in Somerset, where the art of designing
towers was pursued with extraordinary success,
towers were rebuilt from the ground. But the
proportion of towers, with or without spires, which
have been heightened to meet the requirements of a

clerestory, is probably in excess of the proportion of towers entirely rebuilt. In the case of heightened towers, the pitch of the older roof of the nave can generally be made out by the retention of its housing slot or weather course in the east wall of the tower. At Gedney, in south Lincolnshire, where the lower part of the tower is of the thirteenth century, the line of the contemporary roof may be traced above the tower arch. Above this is another line, marking the pitch of a new roof, made when the arcades were rebuilt in the fourteenth century. The clerestory and the upper story of the tower belong to the fifteenth century. In many instances, however, the flattening of the roof has followed the rebuilding of the tower ; and in these the old weather course will be found on the east face of the tower, above the present roof, as in the south aisle at St Mary's, Leicester. Here the roof was probably flattened in the fifteenth century, when the tower and spire were completed.

§ 33. West doorways are frequently found in towers ; and often, as at Grantham and Newark, they are of some importance in the design. They are a general feature of the larger towers, although sometimes, as at St Michael's, Coventry, where the nave has a west porch north of the tower, they are insignificant, and were probably intended to be little more than a convenient entrance for building

materials. In Northamptonshire, some of the towers
of the churches of the Nene valley have doorways
covered by shallow porches. The beautiful porch at
Higham Ferrers and that at Raunds are the earliest :
later porches occur at Oundle, Rushden, and Keyston,
the last place being just across the border of Huntingdonshire. These western doorways were sometimes
used as principal entrances to the church, and were
provided with holy-water stoups. But habitually
they were kept closed, and used only on special
occasions for ritual purposes, as in the Palm Sunday
procession, when the clergy and choir entered the
church by the west door. Such entrances would be
a natural feature of large churches, like Kettering,
and are found in the west walls of churches like
Stratford-on-Avon, St Mary Redcliffe's at Bristol,
or Ketton in Rutland, where the tower is central or
in a situation not at the west end of the nave. Where
the west doorway is covered by a projecting porch,
as mentioned above, the design possibly recalls the
western porches or Galilees, found in some of our
larger churches, and on an imposing scale, in certain
districts of France. The word Galilee arises from
the fact that the west porch was the last stage in
the Sunday procession, and the celebrant, entering
it first, symbolised our Lord preceding His disciples
into Galilee after the Resurrection, of which Sunday
was the festival. A regular western building of the

Galilee type is a somewhat rare feature in an English parish church ; but there is one at Melton Mowbray, and at Snettisham in Norfolk there is an open porch, projecting beyond the west wall of the church. In both cases the church has a central tower. At King's Sutton in Northamptonshire, there is a vaulted porch in front of the western tower.

§ 34. It has been said that there are churches of the twelfth century in which the tower was omitted, and a bell-cot above the western gable took its place. Quenington in Gloucestershire, and Barton-le-Street in the north riding of Yorkshire, are good examples. In both cases, a north as well as a south doorway were provided to the aisleless nave, although, at Barton-le-Street, this circumstance has been obscured by a modern restoration. In neither case was there a western door ; and in both the north doorway, which stands on the side nearest the village, has probably been always the main entrance. The reason of the two doorways may have been the exigencies of processions, in which the litany was sung, and the altars of the church sprinkled with holy water. Such processions took place, at any rate in the greater churches, every Sunday, and in monastic churches were partly external, to include the buildings of the cloister. In smaller churches, however, external processions would be of rare occurrence, and two doorways would hardly be provided for this reason alone.   As a rule, the ordinary entrance would lie on the side of the church nearest the approach from the village, which was generally on the south. But this is not invariable; and the favourite entrance, even where a village lay to the north of the church, was on the south side.   There are sometimes signs that one of the doorways may have been appropriated traditionally to the use of the tenants of one of the manors in a parish, or to the parishioners of a chapelry who were bound to attend the mother church on certain feasts in the year.   Thus at Barton-le-Street, the south doorway, lying on the side of the church towards the hamlet of Coneysthorpe, is called the Coneysthorpe doorway.   At Easingwold, in Yorkshire, the north doorway is called the Raskelf door, and was doubtless used by the inhabitants of the chapelry of Raskelf on these special occasions.   At Hungerton, near Leicester, the tenants of each of the four manors in the parish still occupy their own quarter of the nave; and at Churchdown, near Gloucester, the names of the various chapelries of the medieval parish are still applied to divisions of the churchyard.   In cases like this, the doorway nearest to the part of the church appropriated to one or more of these separate bodies of parishioners would naturally be used as well as the main doorway.

§ 35.   In its simplest form, the porch is simply a protection to the doorway which it covers.   The

Fig. 9. St Mary's, Beverley: south porch.

timber porches, often beautiful works of art, which are common in Essex and other timber-growing parts of England and Wales, can hardly have served any very practical use, although, like stone porches, they have side-benches, on which worshippers could rest. But, from the days when the south porch of Canterbury cathedral was resorted to by litigants from every part of the kingdom, the church porch was a common place for the transaction of much secular business. Hence, no doubt, it became a permanent stone structure, usually roofed with wood, but sometimes vaulted, as at Barnack, or covered, as in some of the churches round Doncaster, by a high pitched roof of stone slabs. In many later medieval churches, the size of the porch increased, and it was vaulted with elaborate ribbed ceilings, or, as at Lavenham in Suffolk, with fan vaulting. There may sometimes have been, as there was at Canterbury and possibly at Bradford on Avon, an altar in the porch. At South Pool in Devon, the bench which runs along the east wall is raised in the middle, and forms an altar table. A broad south aisle was built in the fifteenth century, but was stopped at the east wall of the porch. A small window, now filled in, directly above the altar, commanded a view of the aisle and the south altar of the chancel from the porch, and was closed on the side of the aisle by an iron grille. Such altars, however, must have been very rare. One may suggest that the altar at South

Pool contained relics, on which oaths were taken by
those who came to the porch to settle business or
disputes which might be terminated by mutual
agreement, without being brought before the regular
courts.

§ 36. From the fourteenth century onwards,
porches with an upper story became common, and it
is certain that much miscellaneous business may
have been transacted in the chamber on the upper
floor. This chamber, so frequently called a 'priest's
room,' was used for several purposes. It was sometimes a chapel of the church. The north porch at
Grantham was either rebuilt or extended northward
in the fourteenth century : the lower story was
vaulted, and the long upper chamber became the
chapel in which the principal relics belonging to the
church were preserved. Stairways were provided in
each of the outer corner-turrets, one for those
ascending to venerate the relics, the other for those
descending, so that a free circulation was assured for
devotees who visited the chapel on feast days. In
addition, a window was made in the wall above the
north door, through which the relics could be
exhibited to worshippers inside the church. The
vaulting was broken down at a later period, and the
two stages combined into one. The south porch also
has an upper chamber, which in later days, like so
many similar chambers, contained the library of the

church. It was probably appropriated to the church-watcher, sometimes the deacon attached to the church, who slept there, and, from a small inner window which projects slightly from the wall, could gain a view of most of the interior of the building. In such

Fig. 10. Cirencester: south porch.

a case the watcher's room would probably also be used as the treasury of the church. The magnificent south porch at Cirencester, in three stages, has fan vaulting in the ground story: the upper rooms were used by the trade guilds of the town, and still form the Guildhall. The close connexion of the guilds with the

religious life of the place made the church their
natural meeting-place ; and their annual meetings
were very generally held in the chapels where they
maintained services in their parish church. The porch
at Cirencester is called the Vice, a corruption of the
word parvise (the Latin *parvisus* = *paradisus*) which
is commonly, though inaccurately, applied to these
storied porches. Among the splendid storied porches
of the later middle ages may be mentioned those at
Thaxted in Essex, Beccles in Suffolk, and Sall in
Norfolk. The upper story of one of the porches at
Sall contains a piscina, and was probably a chapel.

§ 37. It has been noted that there was occasionally
an altar on the first floor of a tower. One still remains
in place at St Michael Penkivel, near Truro, where the
church was appropriated to a college of four chantry
priests, and was rebuilt early in the fourteenth century.
Certain indications have lately been found of another
at Tansor, near Oundle: the conversion of this tower
chamber into a chapel explains the otherwise pointless
addition of a stair at the south-east angle of the tower,
which seriously weakened the fabric. While the term
'priest's chamber,' as applied to the room over the
porch, is by no means accurate, it is probable that
such a room may sometimes have been used by a
chantry priest, or as has been said, by the deacon who
occasionally assisted the incumbent of a church. The
most curious instance of a habitation in connexion

with a church is at Terrington St John's, in the
Norfolk marshland, where the tower stands at some
distance west of the south aisle, and is connected with
it by a two-storied building, divided into chambers.
There seems little reason to doubt that this dark and
uncomfortable, but moderately roomy structure, with
the first floor of the adjoining tower, was occupied by
the curate who served the church. It is well, however,
to look askance on the usual traditions which have led,
for example, to the confident statement that the porch
chambers at Grantham were the vicarages of the two
rectorial portions of the church. Statements, also, with
regard to the defensive use of church towers must
carefully be guarded against, with the proviso that, in
certain districts, there are indications that such an use
was made of them. In some of the churches of north-
west Yorkshire, from the end of the twelfth century
onwards, towers were built with a strength which
indicates that they might become strongholds in time
of warfare; and there is positive evidence that the
tower of Bedale church, in a district much exposed
to the inroads of Scottish invaders, was intended to
receive on occasion a body of defenders. The same
thing is true of fortified towers, like that at Newton
Nottage, on the coast of South Wales. In towers,
again, like those of Llywel and Llanfihangel-Cwm-Du
in Breconshire, and Llanfair-ar-y-Bryn in Carmar-
thenshire, the external construction speaks clearly of

the uses to which such towers might be put in time
of war, while the strong barrel vaults of the ground
floors, the ample planning of the turret stairs, and the
presence in one case, till recent times, of a fire-place on
the first floor, are further indications which support
the idea.

§ 38. It should not be forgotten that a porch was
occasionally used as the foundation of a tower. There
is a good example of a northern porch tower at
Cromhall in Gloucestershire and of a southern porch
tower at Norbury in Derbyshire; but the finest instance
is probably the south tower and spire of Donington
in south Lincolnshire. The south porch at Fowey
in Cornwall is virtually a low tower. It was merely
custom and tradition which made the west tower a
nearly invariable feature in most districts of England
during the greater part of the middle ages. It is
obvious that the position of the tower in the plan is
elastic, and we find it, not merely over the crossing of
the transepts, or over a side porch, or at the extremity
of a transept, or as an upward extension of a transeptal
chapel, but also in a position detached from the
church. The beautiful tower of West Walton in
Norfolk is at the entrance to the churchyard, its
ground story forming the gateway. In examples like
this—Fleet and Tydd St Giles, in the same neighbourhood, stand apart in their churchyards—the insecure
nature of the soil probably made the building of a

bell-tower in direct attachment to the church unsafe, and therefore undesirable.

§ 39.   The Norman chancel in England was rectangular in the majority of cases. It was also narrower than the nave, from which it was divided by an arch.   Such arches are almost invariably, until the middle of the twelfth century, round-headed, and are usually low in elevation.   Their character and width, however, vary greatly.   At North Witham the archway is low and narrow, and the arch is unmoulded ; decoration is confined to the impost-blocks from which it springs.   A wide space of wall is left on either side of the opening.   When in the thirteenth century the chancel was enlarged, these spaces were pierced with wide pointed openings, presumably in order to give a better view of the altar from the body of the church.   In north Yorkshire there are a large number of similar chancel arches, the narrowness and plainness of which have sometimes induced antiquaries to class them as Saxon. Saxon in affinity they may well be ; but at Scawton on the Hambleton hills, where one of them occurs, and the wall on either side is pierced with late Norman openings, we know that the church was built in 1146. At Bracebridge, near Lincoln, where there is a fairly lofty and narrow chancel arch of early character and uncertain date, there are openings, apparently later than the rest of the work, at the sides.   These openings are not carried down to the ground in any of the cases mentioned; and there were probably altars against the wall below them, as was certainly the case at Castle Rising in Norfolk, and Avening in Gloucestershire, where towers occur between nave and chancel. Were such openings invariable, or were they even contemporary with the chancel arch, we might see in them a survival of the triple-arched screen wall of early Saxon times. But they are quite exceptional; and at North Witham both, and at Castle Rising one, are much later than the chancel arch. More frequently the chancel arch is given elaborate architectural treatment, with moulded orders and jamb-shafts, and occupies most of the width, and practically the whole height of the chancel behind. Early Saxon chancel arches were very narrow, as is the case at Escomb and Bradford on Avon—so narrow as to shut off the chancel from the nave. This may have been a survival of the primitive practice which kept, by means of curtains drawn round the canopy of the altar, the consecration of the sacred elements in the Eucharist from the public eye. All through the middle ages, it was customary during Lent to hang a curtain or Lenten veil between chancel and quire; and in many English churches hooks for its support may still be seen. A narrow chancel arch would be much more serviceable for this purpose than a wide one; and its persistent

continuance through the twelfth century may perhaps
be attributed to an early form of this usage.

§ 40. While, in the enlargement of a church, the
nave was usually widened by the addition of aisles,
the chancel was in most cases lengthened, and was
often rebuilt entirely, in order to provide more room
for the stalls of the quire. Thus, at Sandiacre in
Derbyshire, the twelfth century nave and chancel
arch were left untouched, but a splendid chancel was
built in place of the old one during the fourteenth
century. The screen which divided chancel from
nave is gone ; but nowhere can we appreciate better
the practical separation between the parishioners'
portion of the church, and that devoted to the clergy
and quire, which, in churches like this, became almost
as marked as in the monastic and larger collegiate
churches. The lengthened chancel, forming a deep
aisleless projection to the east of the building, was
often treated with great architectural dignity. Nothing
could be more beautiful, from their very simplicity of
design, than the chancels of Mitford in Northum-
berland, or Burgh-next-Aylsham in Norfolk, with their
row of lancet windows in the side walls, and the marked
projection of their string-courses and buttresses. Later
in the thirteenth century, the chancel of Houghton-le-
Spring church, near Durham, gives us another example
from the north of England of spacious planning, with
light admitted through a row of splayed lancets. The

chancel of the collegiate church of St Andrew, Bishop Auckland, enlarged about 1250 or rather later, underwent further alteration not long after, by the substitution of broader two-light openings for the narrower lancets, and of a large mullioned east window for a group of lancets at the east end. In Yorkshire, the chancel of West Heslerton, a simple aisleless church, was lengthened and lightened by a row of lancets not unlike those at Houghton-le-Spring. Further south, the nobility which long lancet windows in bays divided by projecting buttresses, and marked by the strong horizontal lines of string-courses, can give to an architectural composition, is shewn by the chancel of the cruciform church of Hedon, near Hull. Less elaborate, but even more striking by virtue of the height, narrowness, and wide internal splay of the lancet openings, is the chancel of Bottesford in north Lincolnshire. Cherry Hinton, near Cambridge, possibly reaches the high water mark of chancel building which depends for its effect on the arrangement of lancet windows. Acton Burnell in Shropshire, recalls Cherry Hinton in the piercing of its side walls by rows of lancets, with trefoiled rere-arches ; but its east window is a composition of four lights, with geometrical tracery, and marks the transition to an even more imposing type of chancel, in which the side walls are pierced with large traceried windows, and the outside and inside of the building alike are marked by architectural treatment of great beauty, and even splendour. Some of the earliest of these fourteenth century chancels may be found in the east of England. Great Sampford in Essex stands on the border-line between the two centuries. Dennington in Suffolk, a chancel of unequalled beauty, comes within the first quarter of the fourteenth century. Somewhat later is Stebbing in Essex, and a little later still is Great Bardfield. In both of these churches, close to one another, nave and chancel alike were rebuilt, and the arch between them filled with a screen of open tracery in stone. The chancel of Lawford, near Colchester, followed about the middle of the fourteenth century: its chief feature is the licence given to the curvilinear tracery of its windows. Impulse may have been given to this outbreak of energy in the east of England by the great building works undertaken at old St Paul's during the latter part of the thirteenth century: all the examples cited, with the exception of Dennington, are within the bounds of the ancient diocese of London. Further examples which give colour to this view might be cited, such as the chancel which the Cistercians of Tilty, near Dunmow, added to the chapel provided for lay-folk outside their gates about the beginning of the fourteenth century.

§ 41. But even more conspicuous than these are the chancels which are found with some frequency in the ancient and widespread dioceses of York, Lincoln, and Lichfield. The chief features of these are, traceried windows of great beauty of proportion and variety of design, with carefully moulded arches and jambs, boldly projecting buttresses with gables or pinnacles, strings and base courses carried right round the building, often with much elaboration. The internal furniture includes stone piscinae and sedilia, canopied niches on each side of the east window, founders' tombs, and, in some cases, stone Easter sepulchres in the north wall. In almost every case, the masonry is composed of large dressed stones; and the building capacity of the masons reaches a high level of architectural skill. The probable source of the development of masonry and sculpture shewn in these structures is to be found in the architectural work which was going on at York during the last quarter of the thirteenth and first quarter of the fourteenth century. It can be shewn that the York school of masoncraft had some influence at Lincoln. Its influence at Southwell, the southern *matrix ecclesia* of the diocese of York, is undoubted. That it had some influence as far south as the lady chapel of Ely, begun in 1321, is very probable; and the work done there may have reacted in a northward direction. Its influence at Lichfield, during the episcopate of Walter Langton (1296–1321), is more than probable, as Langton was intimately connected with York from his early years till his death. In Yorkshire, the re-building of the cruciform church at Patrington was completed, with the chancel, towards 1350. Earlier than this, probably between 1320 and 1330, the chancels of Patrick Brompton, Kirkby Wiske, and Ainderby Steeple had been built: Croft, near Darlington, and Romaldkirk in Teesdale, belong to much the same period and sphere of influence. Round Southwell and Lincoln, and probably during the same decade, the greatest triumphs of the period were achieved. The founder of the chancel of Hawton, near Newark, died in 1330. The rector who was the founder of the chancel of Heckington, near Sleaford, was presented by the crown in 1308-9, and had licence to found a chantry in the church, probably at the high altar of the rebuilt chancel, in 1328. The chancel of Navenby, near Lincoln, belongs to the same period. At Sib-thorpe, near Newark, a college of chantry priests was founded by stages during the first half of the four-teenth century, and the present chancel seems to have been built about 1330: the founder, as already noted, rebuilt the aisles of his church at Beckingham, a few miles away, before 1347. The architectural likeness between his work at Beckingham and the chancel of Boothby Pagnell, near Grantham, built about 1350, cannot be mistaken. The whole church of Fledborough, north of Newark, was rebuilt, probably about 1343, when a chantry was founded in the lady chapel.

Other Nottinghamshire chancels, the probable date
of which is 1330–40, are Arnold (much rebuilt), Car
Colston, and Woodborough. A certain number of
chancels in Leicestershire, such as that of East
Langton, approximate to the type, without actually

Fig. 11.   Patrington, Yorkshire : north side of chancel and vestry.

reproducing it; but at Cotterstock, in Northamptonshire, where John Giffard, canon of York, founded a
college of chantry priests in 1337, its familiar features
reappear. It reached the diocese of Lichfield—or,

at any rate, Derbyshire—rather later than the period of its general diffusion in the dioceses of York and Lincoln. The chancel of Sandiacre belongs to the decade between 1330 and 1340: Dronfield, which, in proportions and parapet and pinnacle-work, is closely akin to Sandiacre, is later than 1340; Norbury and the handsome chancel of Tideswell are later still, probably 1350–60. The chantry college of Chaddesden, founded in 1355, adds another church, with a smaller and less ambitious chancel, to the group. In the north-western part of Lichfield diocese, the fine vaulted chancel of the collegiate church of Nantwich (1327–33) is probably independent of the general type. There can be no mistake, however, about Halsall in south Lancashire. Here the date, although the later window tracery seems to contradict it, appears to be at latest 1340–50; and the likeness of the internal arrangements to those of the north Yorkshire churches is quite remarkable. In a few instances, the type persisted till much later. The chancel at Claypole, near Newark, was rebuilt about 1400: the fourteenth century nave has a noticeable affinity, in the sculpture of its capitals, to the nave of Patrington. Between 1380 and 1400, the chancel of Burneston, in north Yorkshire, shews distinct traces of the influence of Patrick Brompton and the other neighbouring buildings already mentioned. Burneston, Patrick Brompton, and Croft, were all connected with

St Mary's abbey at York. The convent, as rectoi of
Burneston, may have been responsible for the chancel,
when the whole church was rebuilt. But it must be
repeated that the spread of architecture in parish
churches is due to local piety rather than to the desire
of religious houses to found churches in places from
which they derived their income. The founder of the
chancel of Heckington was not the patron, the rich
abbey of Bardney, but a well-to-do king's clerk, who
was presented to the rectory by Edward II during a
voidance of the abbey. Further, the spread of this
particular type of chancel cannot be referred to
St Mary's abbey or any other monastery, but to the
growth of a school of lay masoncraft which learned its
earliest lessons among the new buildings of St Mary's
abbey and York minster. As we should expect in a
period which was so fruitful in good work, isolated
types of almost equal beauty, the result of original
local skill, constantly make their appearance. Such
are the chancels of North Luffenham in Rutland, or of
Hodgeston in Pembrokeshire—the latter, no doubt,
one of the fruits of that movement in the diocese of
St David's, to which bishop Henry Gower (1328–47)
gave a powerful impulse.

§ 42. The aisleless chancel survived as a favourite
feature of the plan all through the middle ages. The
aisled nave, with the deep aisleless chancel beyond, is
beautiful in plan and elevation alike; and hardly any

Fig. 12. Walpole St Peter : from S.E.

of the great Norfolk churches is so satisfactory in
effect as the fourteenth century church at Tunstead,
or the great fifteenth century church of Walpole St
Peter, where the rebuilding of the chancel followed
that of the nave.   The wealthy lay folk of East Anglia
naturally took charge of the repair of the nave as their
own part of the church.   The rectors, monastic or
otherwise, were less active about the chancel.   The
result is that the uniform magnificence of Walpole St
Peter is by no means found everywhere.   The small
vaulted thirteenth century chancel at Blakeney in
north-east Norfolk, is quite out of proportion to the
large fifteenth century nave and west tower.   The
magnificent church of Sall, near Aylsham, was entirely
rebuilt in the fifteenth century; but the proportions of
the chancel are very modest compared with the gigantic
nave.   Lavenham in Suffolk has one of the most ornate
naves of the later part of the fifteenth century, and a
tower of great height.   The fourteenth century chancel,
however, was kept, and, although chapels were added
to it on the north and south, the eastern bay is insignificant in proportion and rough in masonry when
contrasted with the nave.   A similar disparity, not of
style but of design, exists between the nave and
tower of Stoke-by-Nayland and the less carefully
rebuilt chancel.   The rebuilding of a chancel may
occasionally indicate that monastic impropriators
neglected their duties, until they were compelled to

repair.   The hastily rebuilt chancel at Harringworth
in Northamptonshire, where Elstow abbey was rector,
is in striking contrast to the earlier nave, and may
perhaps be explained in this way.   Croyland abbey
had to attend to its duties at Wellingborough in 1383,
and the present aisled chancel is the result.   At
Walpole St Peter the church was evidently lengthened
eastwards.   The parishioners were probably allowed
to pull down the old chancel when they built their
new nave, and to encroach on its site: they naturally
would contribute towards the new chancel, and this
may account for the unusual splendour of the whole
design.

§ 43.   Medieval sacristies attached to chancels,
and especially to aisleless chancels, are common,
and are in most cases on the north side, with a
door in the north wall close to the altar.   Good
examples of an ordinary kind are at Islip and Aldwinkle St Peter in Northants.   There is a fourteenth
century sacristy at Willingham, near Cambridge, with
a vaulted ceiling.   The vaulted vestry at Burford
is of the fifteenth century.   Generally the sacristy
contained an altar, as at Claypole and Westborough,
between Newark and Grantham; and it is certain
that the sacristies of several of the beautiful chancels
already alluded to, as at Hawton, had their altars,
which might be used occasionally for mass, but would
in any case be useful for laying out and folding up

vestments before and after service. The sacristy at
Heckington is of two stories, the lower probably
intended to be a bone-hole. At Halsall there is
a handsome doorway, west of the founder's tomb,
through which a chantry chapel is entered: this
may have been a sacristy in the first instance. Large
sacristies of two, and even three stories are found.
The upper room or solar, as at Raunds in Northants,
Wath, near Ripon, and other places, was sometimes
provided with a window opening into the chancel,
and may have served, like the solar of the south
porch at Grantham, as the treasury of the church and
a room for the deacon or church watcher. But that
these upper rooms may have been provided as extra
chantry chapels is also probable. The very interesting
vestry building between Peterhouse and its appropriated church of Little St Mary's at Cambridge seems
to have contained the chantry chapel of John Wark-
worth, master of Peterhouse, on its upper floor: there
is also a piscina in the small lower sacristy, which
stands above a bone-hole. The originally very similar
building between St Benet's church and Corpus
appears to have had chantry chapels on both floors.
Perhaps the best example of a two-storied sacristy is
the semi-octagonal building, vaulted on both floors, at
the east end of the north chancel aisle at Long Sutton,
Lincolnshire. This is an exceptional situation; but
there was no fixed place for the sacristy. Often, as

at Darlington or as the vaulted vestry at Rushton,
Northants, it is on the south side of the chancel.   In
certain places, as at St Peter Mancroft in Norwich,
and Lavenham in Suffolk, it projects from the east
wall of the church, below the east window, and is
entered by a doorway at one or both sides of the
altar.   Sometimes, again, as at Sawley and Tideswell
in Derbyshire, the altar was brought forward from
the east wall, and provided with a stone screen wall
or reredos, the space between which and the east wall
became the sacristy.   A similar screening off of the
east end of an aisle is found, for example, at Rushden
and Higham Ferrers in Northants : in these cases, it
has been effected without interfering, as at Tansor,
with the proper spacing of the aisle.

§ 44.   Three features which are specially noticeable
in the planning of the aisleless chancel may be mentioned here.   The first is the very usual provision of
squints, or oblique piercings, through the backs of the
responds of the chancel arch.   One object of these
was to enable the priest, celebrating at the aisle
altar, to see what was going on at the high altar,
if his mass happened to coincide with or overlap
another service.   They would also be of use to the
ringer of the sanctus bell, when the bell-cote was
above the chancel arch, and the rope hung down at
the side, out of sight of the altar.   The second point
is the occurrence of a separate door, for the use of the

priest, in the south wall of the chancel: this was provided in a very large number of cases, and, though usually small, was often treated with some architectural dignity. At Trunch in Norfolk it is covered by a small porch. The third point, which has been the

Fig. 13. Wensley, Yorkshire: chancel and S. aisle from S.E., shewing low side window.

cause of much controversy, is the presence of a window, usually in the south wall of the chancel, and near its west end, the level of which is generally just above the back of the chancel stalls. This is known as a 'low side' window. These windows are not confined to chancels, nor to one side of the chancel only : sometimes, as at Acaster Malbis, near York, and Burton Lazars in Leicestershire, they are on both sides of the chancel ; here and there, as at Gretton, Northants, on the north side only. Their design also varies. Not infrequently separate windows, they are formed quite as often by lowering the sill of a single-light or two-light window, and cutting off the lower from the upper part by a transom or cross mullion. Where this arrangement was adopted, the upper part of the window was glazed, but the lower portion seems generally to have been closed by shutters. Many fanciful explanations, which have little foundation in common sense, have been given for the use of these windows. Most popular has been the idea that they were used by lepers, who could not take part in the common services of the church, but could assist at mass and even be communicated through these windows. This fancy disregards the sanitary precautions of the middle ages, which were excellent and plentiful. We may well believe that the people of Burton Lazars would have been horrified, if they had seen, one Sunday morning at mass, their two low side windows darkened by sufferers from the dreadful disease, for whom a hospital with its chapel was carefully provided in their own village. A very widely accepted theory is that low side windows

were used in connexion with the consecration of
the elements at mass : a small hand-bell may have
been rung at the window, so as to be heard outside
the church, especially where the village lay on the
south side. Churches are comparatively few in which,
as at March or Walpole St Peter, a special cot was
provided for a sanctus bell above the chancel arch.
At Hawstead in Suffolk a sanctus bell remains in
position on the inner side of the chancel screen. In
the aisleless church of Preen in Shropshire, where
the chancel, belonging to a small cell of monks, a
colony from Wenlock, was divided by a screen from
the parochial nave, there is a low side window in the
north wall, just east of the place where the screen
originally stood with an altar against it. The window
has a lowered sill, with a stone seat on either side ;
and its position suggests that it was used for chancel
and nave altars alike. A seat at the window, as at
Morpeth, would have been useful for the server who
rang the bell ; but some think that it may have been
used by the priest in hearing confessions. The
common explanation of any unfamiliar object in
a church is that it had to do with confession ; and
one therefore hesitates to adopt a solution of the
difficulty which is so open to suspicion. But there are
certainly windows which are recessed too deeply to
allow of the sanctus bell being audible through them,
and no existing example affords any real convenience

for confessions. It is difficult, moreover, to explain,
on the sanctus bell or confession hypotheses, why, at
Othery in Somerset, there should be not merely a low
side window in the south chancel wall, but a corresponding opening through the south-east buttress of
the central tower, evidently planned in relation to the
window. Also why, in some examples, is there a hook,
as though for a hanging lamp, in the soffit of the
window-head? Cases of this kind have been explained, with much learning, by the possible use of
the 'low side' window as a place for a lamp, which
was hung there to frighten evil spirits from the
churchyard, and could be trimmed from the outside
by merely opening the shutters. To those who know
anything of medieval thought, this is not unlikely. No
explanation yet advanced is wholly satisfactory. The
difference of opinion leads to the conclusion that the
use of the low side window was not one and invariable,
and that it may have been intended for more than
one use, but the sanctus bell hypothesis appears to
fit the largest number of cases. The fact that cots
for sanctus bells are, as a rule, comparatively late
additions to buildings, should be taken into account
in considering the use of the low side window. In
our own day, it often serves the very practical purpose
of giving additional light to the west end of a very
dark chancel; but this can hardly have been its
original object.

§ 45. The double crypt at Grantham, below the south chapel of the chancel, is not a very usual feature. The entrance to the Grantham crypt was originally by two external doors, which still remain. In process of time, it is not improbable that the relics, which at an earlier date were in the chapel above the north porch,

Fig. 14. St Mary Redcliffe. Bristol: from the south-east.

were translated to the eastern crypt. A stairway, with a very imposing doorway at its head, was made to it from the south side of the chancel in the early part of the fifteenth century. A certain number of crypts of Saxon date still remain beneath chancels:

these, however, are few, and perhaps the last survival of the *confessio* in the English parish church is the aisled crypt at Lastingham, near Pickering. The greater part of a twelfth century crypt, with ribbed vaulting, remains beneath the chancel at Newark. Where the church is built on ground with a steep slope eastward, it is more economical to build the chancel on an open crypt, which also may have its uses as a bone-house when the churchyard is cleared, than to build it on a solid lower stage. This accounts for the crypts at Bedale and Thirsk in Yorkshire, and Madley, near Hereford, which are really lower stories to the chancel, and not subterranean chambers. The Lastingham crypt is also built on an abrupt eastward slope. The site of St Mary Redcliffe at Bristol allowed for the construction of large crypt-chambers on its north side and beneath the lady chapel. Sometimes, as at Hythe in Kent, the floor of the chancel was raised to make room for a crypt below. Such crypts were used as bone-houses, when the churchyard was disturbed to make room for new burials. The crypt beneath the south aisle at Rothwell, in Northampton-shire, contains a collection of bones to which, as to that at Hythe, ill-founded legends have been attached. Both these large bone-holes contain altars, at which masses for the dead were said : there is also an altar in the eastern crypt at Grantham. Sometimes, as at Oundle and St Mary Magdalene's, Bridgwater, there

is a small crypt or bone-hole beneath one of the transeptal chapels.   Bone-holes also occur beneath the
east end of an aisle, as at Higham Ferrers in Northamptonshire, and Hallaton in Leicestershire.   At
Burford, St Thomas' chapel, to the west of the south
transept, has its floor raised to give headway to the
vault of the bone-hole below.   A similar bone-hole
is entered from the interior of the south aisle at
Bosham, in Sussex : the altar at the end of the aisle
is raised on a platform above it, as the floor of the
hole is only a little below the level of the aisle.   The
splendid twelfth century crypt at St Mary's, Warwick,
extended beneath the chancel and transepts of the
collegiate church, and is to be classified with the
crypts or lower churches of our Norman cathedrals,
rather than with the less ambitious crypts of our
parish churches.

CHAPTER IV

THE FURNITURE OF A MEDIEVAL PARISH CHURCH: CONCLUSION

§ 46. Our parish churches, as we have them to-day, are stripped of much that made them beautiful. The cold walls, often scraped of all their plaster and whitewash; the windows, glazed with white glass, or with modern glass of very uncertain merit, reveal merely the structural skeleton of the building. The robe of colour with which the interior was clothed is gone; and only fragments here and there remain to tell us of the beauty of the decorative art which was, at the close of the middle ages, at its very highest point. But enough is left to enable us to picture to ourselves the appearance of the interior of an English medieval church, and reconstruct that arrangement of furniture and pictorial decoration which made it so beautiful.

§ 47. To take, first, the features common to nave and chancel alike, the walls of the building were covered with paintings executed on a plaster surface.

Fig. 15.   Patrington, Yorks: interior, looking across
nave from south transept.

As might be expected, the best remains of such paintings are to be found in districts where the churches are built of rubble, and the plaster covering, necessary to the internal wall-surface, afforded the fullest field for this form of decoration. There are numerous and beautiful examples in Sussex and Surrey, from which a good idea may be gained of the general scheme of painting in a medieval church. The earlier wall-paintings, such as those at Copford in Essex, or South Leigh in Oxfordshire, or the probably thirteenth century paintings at Easby in Yorkshire, are stiff in drawing and somewhat crude in colouring. From the earliest times, however, this method of decoration was adopted, and gradually assumed a more independent existence and a more pictorial character. As the history of art advanced, and the demand for special kinds of work increased, the lesser arts, hitherto treated as mere servants of masoncraft, began to strike out paths for themselves. The painters at Pickering in Yorkshire or at Raunds in Northamptonshire, treated the walls on which they worked as the backgrounds of strong and brightly coloured designs bearing no relation to the architectural divisions of the building. Where the space to be covered was limited, like the wall between two aisle windows, the treatment was more restrained : in these positions there occur, as at St Breage in Cornwall, panel pictures of saints. In the north aisle at Kettering

there is a faded picture of St Roch, the blue background of which, studded with gold stars, is a
beautiful example of medieval colour.   But the
general treatment pursued by the later medieval
painters, in their subject and figure painting, was
unconfined by architectural limits, and sometimes a
single subject spreads below and round a window.
Above the chancel arch was usually a painting of the
Doom, of which traces remain in many churches,
as at Holy Trinity, Coventry, and (much restored)
at St Thomas, Salisbury.   At Liddington in Rutland
and at Kettering, the Doom seems to have been
extended to the north and south walls of the nave :
there is on the north clerestory wall at Kettering,
a figure of an angel looking towards the middle of
the wall above the chancel arch ; while there are
remains on the south wall at Liddington, of a huge
whale-like figure representing the mouth of Hades.
The subjects represented in these paintings were of
the utmost variety.   A good idea of the beauty of
colour attained by the artists of the fifteenth and
sixteenth centuries may be gained from a study of
the fragmentary figure and pattern paintings at
Cirencester or the important remains at Bloxham.
To the end of the middle ages much pattern and
diaper work was used in painting large surfaces or
filling in backgrounds.   In several Northamptonshire
churches the soffits of arches are covered with reddish

brown scrolls of leafage, at its best most elaborate
and delicate. The shafts in the angles of the tower
at Fairford are painted with a spiral pattern in two
colours, like a barber's pole, and at Fairford and
Burford there are important remains of late diapered
backgrounds. One of the best pieces of fifteenth
century diaper painting known to the present writer
is that above the chancel arch at Llanbedr-ystrad-yw
in Breconshire, which served as a background to
a rood and figures of St Mary and St John.

§ 48. Mural painting, however, was little more
than a complement to the stained or painted windows,
which were the most gorgeous note of colour in the
medieval fabric. There is no more familiar feature
of medieval architecture than the gradual increase
in the size of windows, due to that constant progress
in the science of architectural construction, in which
the timber-roofed parish church followed the vaulted
cathedral. The low round-headed windows of the
twelfth century were followed by the long lancets of
the early thirteenth century. Lancets gradually drew
closer and closer together, and were united with
spherical openings above, until the mullioned window
with its geometrical tracery was formed. The restless
spirit of the medieval craftsman was not satisfied
with tracery imprisoned within geometrical limits :
the enclosing circles and triangles were removed,
and the tracery twined in naturalistic curves in the

head of the window. Then, at the middle of the
fourteenth century, the limit of the imitation of
nature was reached. The Black Death formed a
sudden division between the work of the old school
and the new age, and that formalism in window
tracery began, which lasted for years, and left its
mark on our architecture as late as the days of the
Stewarts. It was long the fashion among those who
saw merely the decline in architectural detail, dis-
tinctive of the 'Perpendicular' style, to speak of the
magnificent achievements of the fifteenth century
masons with an overbearing contempt. As a matter
of fact, fifteenth century builders were gifted with
a power of design, and an ability to plan a parish
church as a whole, unequalled in the previous history
of medieval art. They lost their interest in sculptured
detail, because their main concern was with the broad
contrasts of light, shade, and colour, which their large
windows and high walls afforded—contrasts in which
there was no use for minute detail, and the deep
under-cutting and delicate carving of the earlier
styles became mere waste of time. The great sheets
of coloured glass, in which, as time went on, painting
became of more and more importance, and large
figures beneath tall canopies of white glass took the
place of the smaller subjects and more deeply coloured canopies and grounds of an earlier time, supplied
an effect fully as beautiful as that once given by the

contrasts of bold projections and deep hollows in moulded arches and carved foliage. The mason in no small degree sacrificed his skill to the glazier; but, in the service of the glazier, his power of noble design on a large scale increased. No effect of colour can well surpass that which is still to be seen in some of our late medieval churches—the grisaille windows of the chancel at Norbury in Derbyshire, the good fourteenth century figure glass of the north aisle at Lowick in Northamptonshire, the fifteenth century east window of the south aisle at St Winnow in Cornwall, the fourteenth century Jesse tree, once in St Chad's, and now in St Mary's at Shrewsbury, or the fifteenth century Jesse tree at Llanrhaiadr-yn-Cynmerch, near Denbigh. Some of the parish churches of York are almost as rich in glass as the cathedral itself. But, in those churches which are still so fortunate as to retain nearly all their medieval glass, like All Saints, North Street, at York, St Neot in Cornwall, and Fairford, the lack of the connecting link which the mural paintings between the windows formed in the colour-scheme is sadly felt. At Fairford, in particular, where the wall-painting which remains is not near the windows, the glass, in its frame of cold plastered wall, gives the effect of isolated masses of almost violent colour, which need to be reduced to their proper key by the painting of the intermediate wall surfaces. On the other hand, at Pickering or Raunds, where we have the mural paintings, the glass is wanting. Often, where painting and stained glass have both disappeared, as in the chapel at South Skirlaugh, their necessity to the building forces itself on the attention. Probably, the full value of stained and painted glass in architectural design, and the relations which prevailed at the close of the middle ages between the mason and glazier, can be judged nowhere in Europe better than in King's college chapel at Cambridge.

§ 49. The third source of colour to the church, apart from the stonework and the stained glass, was the woodwork of roofs, screens, and other pieces of furniture. With this must be reckoned also the colour of the stone furniture of the church, the sedilia, canopied tombs, stone reredoses, pulpits, and so on. As a rule, the colouring of the stone, here as upon the walls, has faded away or has been obscured by later coats of plaster or whitewash. Here and there, as at Higham Ferrers, a tomb-canopy keeps not a little of its original brilliance. There is a gorgeous coloured frame, probably much restored, for a reredos in the north chapel at Worstead in Norfolk. The panels of the reredos in the south aisle at Northleach contain certain figures of saints, in faded green, red, and blue. The fine reredoses in the side chapels of St Cuthbert's at Wells have brilliant remains of gilding. But coloured woodwork, which has lost little of its brightness, is fairly common, and, though it has often

been subjected to drastic restoration, is sometimes
almost untouched by time. This type of art reached
its highest point in the churches of East Anglia, in
the great roofs, with their figures of angels at the end
of the hammerbeams or at the foot of the principal
rafters, extending from end to end of the building, in
the canopies of the fonts, like that at Ufford St Mary,
near Woodbridge, and in the rood screens, like that
at Ranworth, its openings fringed with cusping of
gilded plaster, and its panels painted with figures of
saints and archangels, which sometimes, as at Southwold, were set within a raised frame of gilded gesso
work.

§ 50. This setting of colour, towards which stone,
wood, and glass all contributed their share, constituted
the great beauty of the internal effect of a medieval
parish church ; and naturally, the more the various
craftsmen who worked there advanced in skill—their
skill growing in proportion to their opportunity—the
more gorgeous was the effect of the assemblage of
brilliant windows, screens, and pictured walls. The
usual entrance would be through the south porch.
Near the entrance, or, at any rate, near the west end
of the church, stood the font, beneath its canopy.
No piece of church furniture was subject to so much
variety of design as the font ; and the types vary from
perfectly unadorned examples to structures of the
utmost richness   The canopy was sometimes a simple

Fig. 16. Well, Yorkshire: font cover.

cover, which could be moved by hand : often it was
a towering structure, suspended by pulleys from the
ceiling : sometimes it formed a roofed enclosure on
carved uprights, within which the font stood, of stone
at Luton in Bedfordshire, of wood at Trunch in
Norfolk. Some fonts, like the famous one at Little
Walsingham in Norfolk, perhaps the most beautiful
of those on which the seven Sacraments are represented, stand on high stepped platforms: others are on
a low plinth, which is occasionally continued from the
base of a neighbouring column. In fact, the arrangement of fonts is as various as their shape. The rest
of the furniture of the nave would vary. Some of the
East Anglian churches, such as Irstead in Norfolk,
or Dennington and Fressingfield in Suffolk, keep many
of the medieval benches, with narrow seats, backs
with carved lines of open-work, and projecting ledges
which to-day are used for book-rests. The age of
hassocks had not come, and the ledges, narrow and
very roughly carved, would form a very convenient
support for the elbows of worshippers kneeling upon
the rush-strewn floor of the church. Many English
churches were seated with benches of this kind during
the fourteenth and fifteenth centuries. Few parts of
England are without their examples of bench-ends.
Many fine examples remain in Cornwall, as at Launcells, and in Somerset, as at Trull ; and in some
churches, as Down St Mary and Lapford in Devon,

the early sixteenth century bench-ends are almost
complete. Wooden benches, however, do not seem
to have become general till a comparatively late
date, and there was probably little seating accommodation in the earlier churches. The plinths of
columns were sometimes made of some size, as at
Coddington in Notts, to afford seats ; and in some
churches, as Belaugh and Tunstead in Norfolk, and
Cotterstock, Tansor, and Warmington in Northamptonshire, there are stone benches round the inner
walls of various parts of the church, apparently for
the same purpose.

§ 51. At the east end of each aisle, as has been
shewn, there was in every church an altar. This
was enclosed within screens, shutting off, as a rule,
the eastern part of the aisle. The screens remain
at Dennington, where the loft above the rood screen
was continued round them, with fine effect. At
Wolborough in south Devon, the side screens also
project from the main screen ; and, in many cases
where the screens themselves have disappeared, holes
in the adjacent columns, vertical grooves in the bases,
and other similar signs, bear witness to their former
existence. All the side altars of a church would be
fenced in by screens. In large churches, such as
Grantham, there was often more than one chapel in
an aisle : the north and south aisles of the nave at
Grantham contained at least two chapels each. There

were four chapels in the south aisle at Ludlow, three in the north: the transepts each contained two chapels; and, in addition to these, five of the arches of the nave had chapels beneath them, while the altar of the Cross stood at the east end of the nave in front of the tower.

§ 52. A nave like this would be broken up by a great variety of screen-work; for the clear vista from end to end and side to side of a building, so dear to the restorer of the middle of the nineteenth century, formed no part of the medieval ideal. A space, however, would be kept clear near the pulpit, which, at Ludlow, stood west of the first pier from the east of the north arcade. The stone pulpit at Cirencester is in much the same position; at Wolverhampton, it is on the south side of the nave; at Nantwich it is against the north-east pier; at Holy Trinity, Coventry, against the south-east pier of the central tower. The medieval pulpits of Devonshire stand just west of the rood screen; some, like Kenton, on the north; others, like Dartmouth, on the south side of the entrance. The sermon was hardly so prominent a feature in the services of the medieval church as it became at a later date; but many medieval pulpits remain, and those at Wolverhampton and Coventry, in particular, are imposing structures. The regular furniture of the nave was completed by the pulpit. However, there are some other features to notice. Each altar, or, at any rate, each of the more important altars, would have its own piscina: the chantries at the ends of the aisles sometimes had their own sedile or sedilia. On a bracket near, or in a niche behind each altar, would be a figure, carved and painted, of the saint to whom it was dedicated; and before certain altars where a light or lights were maintained there would be hanging lamps or stands for candles according to the endowment. Thomas Sibthorpe, when he founded his chapels at Beckingham, provided for lights before each altar: in the chantry certificates made under the chantry act of Edward VI, many notices are found of stocks of money by which lights were maintained to burn before specified altars. There would be a holy water stoup in the wall, on the right hand as one entered the church: often the stoup is found in the porch. In some of the Norfolk churches—Sall, Cawston, Aylsham, and Worstead are the best instances—the lower part of the tower is screened off from the nave, the screen supporting a floor which forms a ringers' gallery. In the ringers' gallery at Sall there is a kind of crane, by which the cover of the font, which stands close to the west end, is lifted. In a few churches, as at Weston-in-Gordano in Somerset, there are remains of a small gallery above the main doorway of the church. This is sometimes explained as a gallery used on Palm Sunday by the semi-chorus who joined in chanting the processional hymn. Such a gallery might be used by singers or minstrels on special occasions.

§ 53. The transepts, where they occur, were, as has already been said, used as chapels, or divided off into more than one chapel. Little need be said of the chapels on either side of the chancel, as the general arrangement of their altars and furniture was not very different from that of the chancel itself. The quire and chancel were divided from the nave by the rood screen. This important piece of furniture, usually of wood, but sometimes of stone, crossed the chancel arch from side to side; and was often continued, in churches where the chancel arch was omitted, across the west end of the chancel aisles. Where there was a chancel arch, the chancel chapels had their own screens. The rood screen was elaborately carved, and its lower panels were painted with figures of angels, saints, prophets, apostles, and other designs. The uprights dividing the panels were continued upwards on either side of open panels, sometimes treated as tall arched openings, at other times imitating the form of mullioned windows, and were framed into a plinth at the bottom, and a horizontal beam at the top. The central division of the screen was closed by folding doors : on either side of this entrance was sometimes, against the west side of the screen, an altar. At Ranworth in Norfolk the screen altars are enclosed by panels returned from the face

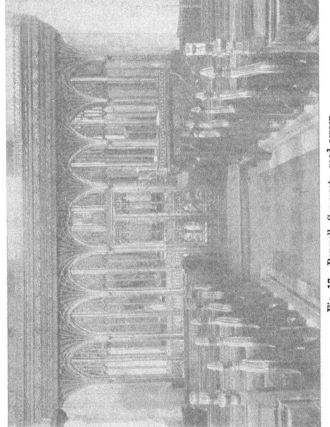

Fig. 17. Banwell, Somerset : rood screen.

of the screen: there are distinct traces of this arrangement at Weston-in-Gordano and other places ; and, at
Lapford and Swymbridge in Devon, there are large
rectangular openings in the traceried panels of the
upper part of the screens, across which painted cloths
seem to have been stretched at the back of the side
altars.   Above the screen, with its floor-beams laid
across the top, and attached to either face by a series
of trusses which formed a deep coved and ribbed
cornice to the screen, was the loft, gallery, or, as it was
often called, the 'solar.' Sometimes, as at Montgomery
and Llanwnog, the screen was double, the floor of the
loft forming a roof to the space between.   This upper
story had a projecting parapet on either side, the
front of which was divided into panels and painted.
It was approached by a staircase, the position of
which varied greatly.   In churches with an aisleless
chancel, the stair was contained in a turret to the
north or south of the chancel arch, which was, if there
was little room for it, sometimes built out into the
adjacent chapel.   At Dennington, however, where the
loft was continued round the screens at the end of
the nave aisles, the staircase is in the south wall of
the south aisle.   At Ropsley, near Grantham, the
stair is in the outer wall of the north aisle, near the
north-east corner ; and the loft was approached by a
bridge thrown across the end of the north aisle.   In
the aisleless church of Little Hereford, near Tenbury,

where there is a very narrow chancel arch, the loft
was approached by a straight stair in the thickness
of the south half of the east wall : a right-angled turn
at the top led straight into the loft. In churches with
aisled chancels, the stair was commonly contained in
a turret projecting from the outer side of the north
or south wall, and there were lofts continued across
all the screens of the chancel and its chapels. At
Llywel in Breconshire, there is a fairly broad straight
staircase at right angles to the loft, contained in a
broad projection from the north wall of the aisleless
nave : this was a favourite arrangement in Wales,
and occurs at Patricio, and, in the more primitive
form of a wooden stair within a projecting window,
at Llanwnog in Montgomeryshire. Wooden stairs
and even ladders to lofts were probably not unusual.
At Totnes the chief approach to the loft of the stone
screen was a stairway in a half-octagon, projecting
into the north part of the chancel, from the head of
which the way lay along the loft of the adjoining
parclose screen. Few lofts, however, remain. The
Totnes loft, which was of wood, is gone. Several
Welsh lofts, owing, no doubt, to their remote position,
escaped destruction when the general dismantling of
rood lofts was carried out in the reign of Elizabeth.
The most magnificent of these are at Patricio in Breconshire, Llanegryn in Merionethshire, Montgomery
and Llanwnog in Montgomeryshire, and Llananno in

Radnorshire. Less beautiful, but remarkable for the
very perfect state of its painted back-board, is the
loft at Llanelieu in Breconshire. But in remote
English places, such as Blackawton, near Dartmouth,
Cotes-by-Stow in Lincolnshire, and Hubberholm in
west Yorkshire, lofts are left in a fair state of perfection.

§ 54. The use of the loft was, it has often been
said, for the deacon to sing the gospel from at high
mass on great festivals. This was certainly the case
with the stone *pulpita* above the quire screens of
collegiate and monastic churches. But, in most
parish churches the stair was so narrow and incon-
venient that certainly the vestments and probably
the temper of the deacon who attempted to climb it
would be easily spoiled. In many lofts, it is true,
there was an altar. The piscina of one remains in
a few churches, as at Little Hereford: there was a
chantry founded in 1349 at one in Grantham church,
where the screen was a large one of stone. But the
habitual use of the loft was as an organ gallery; and
the fine screen at Newark-on-Trent still has at its east
side the rectangular projection which was occupied
by a 'pair of organs.' The rood itself, the great
cross bearing the figure of our Lord with statues of
St Mary and St John upon either side, stood upon
a beam which crossed the chancel arch above the
loft. The beam was, of course, painted, and, in

addition to the statues which it carried, bore sockets
for candles, which were lighted on festival occasions.
The corbels which supported rood beams are sometimes seen : beams themselves, however, do not often
remain. There is a finely painted example of one
at Tunstead in Norfolk ; and another remains at
Cullompton in Devon. Here and there, where the
beam was fixed in the wall, and had to be sawn away,
the end may still be seen. Some screens had no loft :
in these cases the rood frequently stood upon the top
of the screen. In some cases, as at Llanelieu in
Breconshire and Wenhaston in Suffolk, the rood and
its attendant figures were fixed upon a painted board
which formed a back to the loft, and filled the upper
part of the chancel arch. In other places, as at
Hickleton, near Doncaster, and Llanbedr-ystrad-yw,
they were fixed against the wall above the chancel
arch. This would be the case where, as at Hickleton,
the arch was low and narrow, and there was no room
for a separate beam beneath it. No piece of church
furniture is more interesting than the rood screen and
its accompaniments : the variety of local design and of
its arrangements, and the great beauty of the finished
work, make it, of all special topics of ecclesiology,
perhaps the most attractive.

§ 55. It has been said before that the hooks
by which the Lenten veil was suspended west of the
high altar are still to be seen in several churches.

The western part of the chancel was occupied by
the quire, whose stalls were returned along the
back of the screen, the rector's stall being the end
return stall on the south side. Quire stalls in
parish churches were often carved with great re-
finement and beauty : the stalls at Walpole St Peter
have each a stone canopy, formed by recessing panels
in the chancel wall. The finest stalls, with their
hinged seats, rightly called misericords, and wrongly
misereres, are usually to be found in collegiate or
chantry churches, like Higham Ferrers or Ludlow,
where the chantry priests of the Palmers' guild said
their offices together in the high chancel. The stalls
of the chantry college at Fotheringhay are now in the
churches of Tansor and Benefield ; the quire stalls of
St Mary's at Nottingham are in the suburban church
of Sneinton. An excellent instance of the combina-
tion of stalls and rood screen is found in the village
church of Ashby St Ledgers, near Daventry, which
contains a large amount of old woodwork. In the
centre of the quire or, as a gospel-desk, on the north
side of the altar would stand the lectern. The
number of medieval lecterns remaining in England is
not great, the finest being the great brass lectern
given by provost Hacomblen to King's college,
Cambridge. Lecterns in which the desk takes the
form of a bird are sometimes found, as in Norwich
cathedral and at Ottery St Mary.

§ 56. When interest was first revived in ecclesiology, the fashion of raising the quire and
chancel above the rest of the church, by a number
of steps intended to be symbolical, became very
prevalent. This, however, was not in keeping with
medieval practice. It is true that occasionally
chancels were raised high above the rest of the
church. At Walpole St Peter the chancel, rebuilt
in the fifteenth century, was brought up to the
churchyard boundary, and apparently interfered with
a right of way which led round the back of the old
chancel. It was therefore built with a floor raised
high above the nave, and the right of way was
preserved by piercing an arch below. St Stephen's
at Exeter has a chancel built over an archway which
affords access to a narrow street. A church built on
a slope, like Tansor, ascends noticeably from west to
east. But the ascent is contrived, not by means of
flights of steps, but by an inclined plane. As a rule,
floors of churches sloped slightly upwards towards
the altar. A perfectly level floor gives the false
effect in perspective of a downward slope: a floor, on
the other hand, with a gradual upward slope has
a level effect. The floor of the quire was sometimes
elevated by a single shallow step above the floor of
the nave: very generally, it was on the same level:
at St Michael's, Cambridge, the level was slightly
lower. The chancel, again, was a step higher than

the quire, and the altar stood slightly raised upon its
own oblong altar pace.   The levels at Geddington in
Northamptonshire remain much as they were.   The
quire is on a level with the nave : the chancel is
a pace higher, and the altar stands upon its own pace.
An inscription round the foot of the chancel wall
records the making of the pavement (now renewed)
and the *scabella*, by which the foot-paces are almost
certainly implied, of the altar in 1369.   Round the
lower foot-pace of the south chapel is another inscription, apparently of the same date.   In no respect
have modern restorations been so disastrous as in the
altering of original levels, in order to give the altar
the elevation which was supposed by the restorers to
be necessary.

§ 57.   The altar itself, as can be seen from the
many altar-slabs which remain, was a long and fairly
broad stone table : it was usually less than three feet
high, and was covered by a cloth and frontal.   It is
probable that the frontal, like the vestments of the
clergy, followed, in the ordinary parish church, no
very strict sequence of colour according to the seasons.
For festivals the handsomest and newest frontal
and vestments would probably be used.   The altar
was kept fairly low, to make room for the reredos,
which extended across the east wall above the altar,
and below the sill of the east window.   It will be
found that modern restorers, in nine cases out of ten,

have disregarded old English uses, by raising an altar
until its upper surface is close to the sill of the window,
and then by blocking up part, or even the whole of the
window, by reredoses or altar screens of stone or
wood. High reredoses and altar screens were not
unknown, of course, in England; but the ordinary
reredos was a single or double band of carving below
the east window, as at Geddington or Ludlow. At
Stanion in Northants, the string-courses of the east
walls of the chancel and north chapel are raised,
below the east windows, to form frames for mural
paintings or carved retables above the altar. Sculptured tablets were not rare, and indications of their
presence may be traced: in the fourteenth and fifteenth
centuries, the alabaster, dug out of the Chellaston
'plaster-pits,' and worked by the 'plasterers' of
Nottingham, was used, among other purposes, for
such tablets. On the north and south sides of the
reredos the altar was enclosed by curtains hung on
brass rods projecting from the wall or from upright
standards. These curtains, known as riddels, had
sockets for candles at the ends of the rods. They
appear to be derived from the curtains which hung
round the altar canopies of basilican churches, and
were drawn at the consecration of the elements. Probably the reredos, in most churches, was formed by a
painted cloth—that is, a piece of embroidered tapestry
—hung behind the altar, or stretched from the

upright of the one to the upright of the other riddel.
It may be added that the arrangement of cross,
candles and flower vases on a shelf, or even on
several shelves, at the back of the altar, with which
we are so familiar, was not frequent in the middle
ages. The cross was usually the central carved or
embroidered feature of the reredos: one or two
lighted candles were placed upon the altar at mass;
and flowers and sweet smelling herbs would be strewn
at certain seasons on the chancel floor. Richness of
colour and simplicity of furniture were the distin-
guishing features of the medieval altar. There is a
curious ledge upon the back part of the upper surface
of the crypt altar at Grantham: it actually lies *upon*
the altar, and its height, as contrasted with that of the
modern gradine or shelf, affords the same contrast that
there is between the low foot-paces of the medieval,
and the flights of steps of the modern chancel.

§ 58.   The statue of the patron saint stood near
the altar, on a corbel in the wall, in a canopied recess,
or, as at Abbots Kerswell in Devon, where there is
a very large figure of the Virgin, in the jamb of a
window.   In front of the altar, the pyx, or receptacle
for the reserved Sacrament, hung by chains from the
roof: it was covered by an embroidered veil, which was
drawn aside when the pyx was opened. The rest of the
ordinary furniture of the chancel was of a more permanent description.   The piscina and sedilia, which are

frequently of one date and form part of one design, were on the south side of the chancel, forming arched recesses in the wall. The number of sedilia varied from one to three: more than three are seldom found in a parish church. Permanent stone sedilia were usually regarded as part of the regular furniture of the chancel. Occasionally their place was supplied by the lowering of a window sill; but there were also instances, no doubt, in which the sedile or sedilia were simply wooden chairs placed near the south wall of the chancel. The piscina was frequently supplied with an upper ledge for cruets. In the piscina of the south aisle at Hawton, near Newark, there is an inner recess for this purpose on the east side; at Tansor a shallow niche is provided in the head of the arch of the piscina. The drain of the piscina was usually within the wall; but there are a number of twelfth century, and a few later, examples, in which the bowl forms a projection from the wall, and the drain was contained in a detached column, the base of which is frequently united to the foot of the wall. Projecting bowls are common, with drain-holes which slant downwards into the wall. A piscina is sometimes found in the sill of a window: one at Grantham is fitted with a removable drain, and there are other such examples. A drain in the chancel floor is sometimes found, usually of a rather early period. In addition to the piscina, most churches contain

plain almeries or cupboards, rectangular recesses
with rebates for wooden doors : these are generally
in the north or east wall of the chancel.

§ 59.   More exceptional—indeed, very uncommon
—as a piece of furniture, was the permanent Easter
sepulchre, which usually was on the north, but sometimes on the south of the chancel. This was the place to
which the Host was carried on the evening of Maundy
Thursday, and left until Easter even : it was symbolical
of the sepulchre of our Lord, and the services which
took place in connexion with it were sometimes of a
somewhat dramatic character.   A permanent Easter
sepulchre, like those at Hawton and Heckington, was
a luxury.   These, and the sepulchre at Navenby,
have carvings referring to the story of the Resurrection, and in the lower panels are represented the
guards at the tomb.   The recess at Hawton, forming
a triple opening, has an inner recess at the back,
which could be shut and locked.   At Heckington and
Navenby the recesses are merely single cupboards,
surrounded by elaborate carving.   Frequently, an
almery was used for the purpose; and where, as at
Frating in Essex, Claypole in Lincolnshire, or Sefton
in Lancashire, an almery is treated with special care,
as, for example, with a floral hood-mould, this
special use is indicated.   There may also have been
removable sepulchres of wood: a piece of furniture
which remains at Cowthorpe in Yorkshire, is said to be

Fig. 18. Hawton, Notts.: Easter sepulchre.

one. Another was made for St Mary Redcliffe, Bristol,
in 1440.   Certainly, the sepulchre was often a tem-
porary arrangement, like the *reposoir* in a French
church to-day.   Thomas Meyring of Newark directed
his burial to take place 'where the sepulchre of our
Lord was wont to be set up at Easter.'   A founder's
tomb near an altar was also used for the sepulchre, the
receptacle for the Host being probably placed inside
the tomb-recess or against it.   At Sibthorpe near
Newark, the small sepulchre is immediately above
the founder's tomb : this was probably the case at
Fledborough.   At Owston, near Doncaster, a tomb-
recess in the north chancel wall is often called the
Easter sepulchre, and a projecting stone at one side
of it is pointed out as a stone for the watcher who
kept guard over the tomb at Easter.   The majority
of Easter sepulchres which are left belong to the
fourteenth century.   The imposing structure at Northwold in Norfolk, which is on the south of the chancel,
is of the fifteenth century, and, in at least one example,
at Wymondham in Norfolk, also on the south side,
there are details which approach the Renaissance
period.   The frequent identity of the founder's tomb
with the Easter sepulchre, for which there is docu-
mentary evidence, is proved further by the tombs of
the rector and vicar, under whose auspices, in the
second quarter of the sixteenth century, the chancels
of South Pool and Woodleigh churches in south

Devon were restored.   These are vaulted recesses
north of the altar, containing table tombs with
effigies, and a large amount of florid carving, which
shews signs of Renaissance influence.   On the wall at
the back of either tomb are sculptures dealing with
the burial and resurrection of our Lord, which clearly
point to the use of the tombs at Easter, and justify
the name of Easter sepulchre, frequently applied to
them.   A third tomb of rather later date is at West
Alvington, in the same neighbourhood: its details
were suggested by South Pool and Woodleigh, but
the brasses of the back wall are gone, and its
inclusion in the list of Easter sepulchres is doubtful.
There is a curious late thirteenth century piece of
work, projecting inwards from the north wall of the
chancel at Twywell, near Kettering.   A tomb-recess
forms the lowest stage; above this is a double almery,
which may have been an Easter sepulchre, and above
this, again, is a sloping stone desk with a book-rest
for the reader of the gospel.   Stone gospel-desks are
found in a few Derbyshire churches, like Crich, Spondon, and Etwall; and in a few other rare instances.   A
founder's tomb is, of course, by no means an invariable
feature of a chancel.   The natural place for the burial
of the founder of a chantry would be close to the altar
where his chantry was celebrated; and often, as at
Grantham, the presence of a tomb in an aisle wall
indicates the existence of a chantry altar near that spot.

§ 60. The sacristy has been referred to in the
previous chapter; and with this description of the
furniture of the chancel, our account of the English
parish church is nearly come to an end. Few persons
who are in the habit of visiting parish churches will
fail to meet with exceptional or unique features.
For example, in the north wall of the chancel at
Scawton in north Yorkshire, there is a long oblong
trough, with a drain in the wall behind it, the use
of which is difficult to conjecture. At Tunstead in
Norfolk, there is a narrow platform behind the altar,
the whole width of the east wall. At its south end
is a stair from the floor of the chancel; and near
the stair is a door leading into a chamber below the
platform. This narrow room, far too small for a
sacristy, is lighted by a grating in the floor of the
platform. It is supposed that this was an arrangement for the exhibition of relics. At Tanfield, near
Ripon, there is a little cell-like recess in the wall
between the chancel and north chapel, with a window
commanding the altar. The problems which are set
by these details bring us by degrees into relation with
the whole of medieval life; and the history of the
parish church becomes an important part of the social
history of the parish. The magnificent tombs of the
Marmions at Tanfield also recall to us an artistic
feature of the parish church which opens out a wide
field, and can be dealt with here only so far as the

tombs themselves afford evidence as to the date of the part of the church in which they occur.

§ 61. The actual development of the parish church comes to an end with the Reformation. The building of great churches, cathedral and monastic, ceased with the suppression of the monasteries. The suppression of the chantries, and the new doctrines which it symbolised, did away with one object which had been a powerful consideration with the lay benefactor of parish churches. Henceforward the best work of those English masons who, in every county, had for generations shaped the course of medieval art, and, with it, the best work of the wood-carvers and glaziers, is found in private houses. In the early part of the seventeenth century, under the influence of Laud, much restoration and rebuilding was done. Wood-carvers filled many churches with furniture of great beauty and historical value. Churches like St John's at Leeds, or the little chapel of Carlton Husthwaite in Yorkshire, are, in stone and woodwork alike, complete examples of the work of this period. Brancepeth, Sedgefield, and Eaglescliffe in Durham; Burneston in north Yorkshire; and, above all, Croscombe in Somerset, contain wooden furniture which one would not willingly exchange for medieval work. But, in spite of the richness and picturesqueness of seventeenth century woodwork, the art of the Laudian revival had no power to strike out new lines

for itself. The chancels of Astley Abbots in Shropshire, Kelmarsh in Northamptonshire, and Barsham
in Suffolk, interest us by their quaint adaptation of
Gothic detail: they tell us nothing new. The art of
the mason, as regards the parish church, is exhausted.

§ 62.   At a later date, Wren built parish churches
with an extraordinary elasticity of style and plan. But
the study of Wren's plans is simply the study of the
plans of an individual architect: they are the outcome
of his relation to the fashions of his day, and his
unrivalled capacity for dealing with them.   He established firmly the use of a modified Palladian style in
church architecture, which his successors imitated
until nothing further could be done with it.   But,
when we look at his churches, we never can forget
the architect behind them.   St Martin's-in-the-Fields
and St Mary-le-Strand, by Gibbs; St Philip's at Birmingham, by Archer, fine churches though they are,
fall short of his designs; and we instinctively compare
and contrast their plan and elevation with the models
supplied by Wren.   In the medieval parish church,
on the other hand, the individual architect had no
place; the whole artistic activity of an age was represented; the builder was an original artist, and a
member of a nation of artists; and the development of
the parish church was the work of a national interest,
not merely confined to one highly specialised pro-
fession.   When the Gothic revival came in the early

nineteenth century, it was thought that medieval art
was once more re-born.   But, when we look to-day at
the scholarly and often extremely beautiful work of
artists like Pugin, Sir Gilbert Scott, Street, Pearson,
Butterfield, Bodley, or the younger Gilbert Scott, we
still feel the force of individual design and style rather
than the force of a great collective movement.   All
these, like Wren, have added individual contributions
to church planning and decoration; but their art is
a by-path of national life, and is merely the result of
a purely individual type of thought.

§ 63.   At the same time, to say this is not to
belittle post-Reformation church architecture.   It is
simply to point out the contrast between the work of
the architect and the work of the medieval mason,
between a sporadic development of art, and a development which was general in every part of the country.

But, while the work of later generations differs in
quality and spirit from that of the medieval craftsman,
while it is necessarily more sophisticated and less
spontaneous than his, no greater mistake can be made
than to drive it out of our churches.   The Reformation
and Cromwell have been made responsible for much
destruction : yet no one has destroyed so light-
heartedly as the modern restorer, in his efforts to
bring back churches to what is called their 'original
state.'   To-day, people are waking up to the value of
post-Reformation masonry and furniture.   They realise

that when an eighteenth century church is swept away, and a handsome building, in an eclectic Gothic style, decked with the best products of modern arts and crafts, rises in its place, the advantage is questionable. Not merely does much good furniture inevitably perish, but a link with the past is destroyed. Eighteenth century pews may not be altogether suited to a fifteenth century church ; but they remind us at any rate that the fabric in which they stand has a continuous history. The age which produced them followed its own taste and worked on its own lines, and did not merely strive after an ideal of harmonious imitation. Not only the work of recent centuries has been touched, but medieval work has been altered : screens have been mutilated and removed, old glass has been destroyed, even whole fabrics have been rebuilt with very slight regard to their earlier plan. It can never be impressed too strongly upon the average Englishman that, quite apart from their religious associations, the parish churches of this country form, as a body, one of the most remarkable historical monuments which any European nation possesses. We may regret, perhaps, that past generations have tampered with them ; but for that very reason we should hesitate to tamper with them ourselves, or to replace incongruous work of the past by imitative work of our own. We may well use our individual energy and our new ideas in adding to their number; but our treatment of the older work, where it positively calls for renewal, should be tender, conservative, and self-effacing. The excellence of the medieval mason's work consists largely in his avoidance of self-consciousness, in its perfectly natural and spontaneous feeling : if we attempt to impose our individuality upon his work, we are in danger of supplying to future and, it may be hoped, wiser generations a contrast from which they will not fail to draw a melancholy profit.

BIBLIOGRAPHICAL NOTE

Books exclusively devoted to the subject of the English parish church are few in number, and generally are in the form of descriptions of the churches of special districts, or of monographs on individual churches.

1. Among the older books in which special attention is paid to parish churches, the following may be mentioned:

BLOXAM, M. H., *Principles of Gothic Ecclesiastical Architecture*, 11th ed., 2 vols., London, 1882.

BRANDON, J. R. and J. A., *Parish Churches*, London, 1888. [Perspective views, ground plans, and short descriptions.]

ECCLESIOLOGICAL [Cambridge Camden] SOCIETY, *A Hand-Book of English Ecclesiology*, London, 1847.

NEALE, J. P., and LE KEUX, J., *Views of the most interesting collegiate and parochial churches in Great Britain*, 2 vols., London, 1824–5.

PARKER, J. H., *Introduction to the study of Gothic Architecture*, 12th ed., Oxford and London, 1898.

RICKMAN, T., *An attempt to discriminate the styles of English Architecture*, 7th ed., Oxford and London, 1881.

WICKES, C., *The spires and towers of the mediaeval churches of England*, London, 1859.

2. More modern works, in which the development of the ground plan is treated as part of the general subject, are:

BOND, F., *Gothic Architecture in England*, London, 1905.

BROWN, G. BALDWIN, *The Arts in Early England*, vol. II, London, 1903.

PRIOR, E. S., *A history of Gothic art in England,* London, 1900.

SCOTT, G. G., *An essay on the history of English Church Architecture,* London, 1881.

3.   Among volumes dealing with special districts, the following may be mentioned:

BUCKLER, G., *Twenty-two churches of Essex,* London, 1856.

COX, J. C., *Notes on the churches of Derbyshire,* 4 vols., Chesterfield and London, 1875–9.

CRANAGE, D. H. S., *An architectural account of the churches of Shropshire,* Wellington, 2 vols.

MCCALL, H. B., *Richmondshire Churches,* London, 1909.

NORTHAMPTON, *Architectural notices of the churches of the Archdeaconry of,* London, 1849.

SHARPE, E., *An account of the churches visited during the Lincoln excursion of the Architectural Association,* London, 1871.

SHARPE, E., and others, *Churches of the Nene Valley,* London, 1880.

WILSON, F. R., *An architectural survey of the churches in the Archdeaconry of Lindisfarne,* Newcastle-on-Tyne, 1870.

4.   Books upon individual churches cannot be mentioned here, nor can any detailed list be given of the numerous valuable articles in such publications as *Archaeologia* and the *Archaeological Journal.* Some of the most enlightening work upon the subject is to be found in the papers contributed by the late J. T. Micklethwaite to the transactions of various societies. Those on Saxon churches in vols. LIII and LIV of the *Archaeological Journal,* and the plans contributed by him to J. W. Walker's *History of All Saints, Wakefield* (Wakefield, 1888), may be specially mentioned.

5.   Books on the subject of church furniture are numerous. The most comprehensive modern handbook on the subject is J. C. Cox and A. Harvey's *English Church Furniture,* London,

1907. More detailed treatment of separate articles of furniture is given in F. Bond's *Screens and Galleries, Fonts and Font-Covers*, etc., volumes of a series now in course of publication. J. T. Fowler's edition of *The Rites of Durham* (Surtees Society, 1903), and Rock's *Church of our Fathers* edited by G. W. Hart and W. H. Frere (4 vols., London, 1903–4), are a mine of information on points connected with church services and furniture.

6. The historical aspect of the parish church is treated excellently by E. L. Cutts, *Parish Priests and their People in the Middle Ages* (London, 1898). But, to gain an adequate knowledge of this side of the question, the study of original documents is necessary, and chiefly of the contents of episcopal registers. Of these invaluable texts some have been printed in full, and of others there are printed abstracts, but the vast majority remain in manuscript. The fullest printed series is the *Exeter Episcopal Registers* (ed. F. C. Hingeston-Randolph), covering the period 1258–1455 : the York registers from 1216 to 1285 (ed. J. Raine and W. Brown for the Surtees Society), and the Hereford registers from 1275 to 1327 (ed. W. W. Capes and others for the Cantilupe and Canterbury and York Societies) are also full and accurate editions. Much information with regard to the foundation of chantries and other important subjects may be obtained from the Calendars of the Patent Rolls and of Letters from the Papal Registers, published under the direction of the Master of the Rolls. The Chantry Certificate Rolls and Inventories of Church Goods drawn up between 1547 and 1549 are also sources of great value : these have been printed for some counties, but the greater number are still unpublished.

J. C. Cox and R. M. Serjeantson's *History of the Church of the Holy Sepulchre, Northampton* (Northampton, 1897) may be cited as a model history of a parish church. The arrangement of the topographical sections of the various Victoria County Histories makes it possible to study the history of a large number of churches in company with their architecture.

INDEX

Abbots Kerswell, Devon, 122
Abingdon, Berks., 33
Acaster Malbis, Yorks., 92
Acton Burnell, Salop, 79
Adlingfleet, Yorks., 19
Ainderby Steeple, Yorks., 82
Aldwinkle St Peter, Northants., 88
Alveley, Salop, 36
Alvington, West, Devon., 127
Arnold, Notts., 83
Arundel, Sussex, 37
Ashby St Ledgers, Northants., 118
Astley Abbots, Salop, 130
Auckland St Andrew, Durham, 79
Avening, Glouces., 77
Aylsham, Norfolk, 111
Aysgarth, Yorks., 30

Banwell, Som., 113
Bardfield, Great, Essex, 80
Barnack, Northants., 4, 53, 70
Barsham, Suffolk, 130
Barton-le-Street, Yorks., 67, 68
Barton-on-Humber, Lincs., St Peter's, 54
Bath, Som., cathedral priory, 35
Battlefield, Salop, 28
Beccles, Suffolk, 73

Beckingham, Lincs., 21, 22, 33, 82, 111
Bedale, Yorks., 74, 96
Bedminster, Som., 49
Belaugh, Norfolk, 109
Benefield, Northants., 118
Berkeley, Glouces., 34
Beverley, Yorks., St Mary's, 69
Beverstone, Glouces., 36
Biggleswade, Beds., 33
Birmingham, Warwicks., St Martin's, 31 ; St Philip's, 130
Blackawton, Devon, 116
Blakeney, Norfolk, 87
Bloxham, Oxon., 101
Boothby Pagnell, Lincs., 82
Bosham, Sussex, 97
Boston, Lincs., 31, 36, 62
Bottesford, Lincs., 79
Boughton, Northants., 30
Boxgrove, Sussex, priory church, 35
Bracebridge, Lincs., 76, 77
Bradford-on-Avon, Wilts., 70, 77
Bradwell-juxta-Mare, Essex, St Peter's on the Wall, 2, 3
Brancepeth, Durham, 129
Branston, Lincs., 9, 10, 15, 58
Bridgnorth, Salop, 29
Bridgwater, Som., St Mary Magdalene's, 96

Bridlington, Yorks., priory church, 17
Bristol, St Mary Redcliffe, 48, 49, 66, 95, 96, 126
Brixworth, Northants., 4, 53, 54, 55, 56
Bunbury, Cheshire, 28
Burford, Oxon., 35, 42, 43, 44, 45, 48, 49, 88, 97, 102
Burgh-next-Aylsham, Norfolk, 78
Burneston, Yorks., 84, 85, 129
Burnsall, Yorks., 30
Burton Lazars, Leices., 92

Caistor, Lincs., 58
Cambridge, Clare college, 38; Corpus Christi college, 31, 89; Jesus college chapel, 38, 39; King's college chapel, 105, 118; Michaelhouse, 38; St Peter's college, 34, 38, 89; Trinity Hall, 38; St Benedict's, 89; St Botolph's, 35; St Edward's, 38; Little St Mary's, 34, 38, 89; St Michael's, 38, 119
Canterbury, Kent, cathedral, 4, 70; St Martin's, 2
Car Colston, Notts., 83
Carlton Husthwaite, Yorks., 129
Carlton-in-Lindrick, Notts., 57
Castle Rising, Norfolk, 77
Cawston, Norfolk, 111
Chaddesden, Derby, 38, 84
Chellaston, Derby, 121
Cherry Hinton, Cambs., 79
Chesterfield, Derby, 32, 33, 41
Chipping Norton, Oxon., 32
Chipping Sodbury, Glouces., 32
Churchdown, Glouces., 68
Cirencester, Glouces., 39, 40, 41, 48, 49, 72, 73, 101, 110
Claypole, Lincs., 84, 88, 124

Cleobury Mortimer, Salop, 36
Clovelly, Devon, 28
Coddington, Notts., 109
Coln St Denis, Glouces., 56
Coneysthorpe, Yorks., see Barton-le-Street
Copford, Essex, 100
Cotes-by-Stow, Lincs., 116
Cotterstock, Northants., 28, 37, 83, 109
Coventry, Warwicks., Holy Trinity, 45, 48, 49, 101, 110; St Michael's, 45, 46, 47, 49, 65
Cowthorpe, Yorks., 124
Crediton, Devon, 32
Crich, Derby, 127
Croft, Yorks., 36, 82, 84
Cromhall, Glouces., 75
Croscombe, Som., 36, 129
Croyland abbey, Lincs., 14, 88
Cullompton, Devon, 117

Darlington, Durham, 90
Dartmouth, Devon, St Saviour's, 110
Deerhurst, Glouces., 54, 55
Dennington, Suffolk, 80, 108, 109, 114
Dereham, West, Norfolk, abbey, 11, 12
Donington, Lincs., 75
Down St Mary, Devon, 108
Dronfield, Derby, 84
Durham, cathedral, 8

Eaglescliffe, Durham, 129
Earl's Barton, Northants., 53
Easby, Yorks., 100
Easingwold, Yorks., 68
Elm, Cambs., 59
Elmley, Worces., castle chapel, 29

Elstow abbey, Beds., 88
Ely, Cambs., cathedral, 6, 59, 81
Escomb, Durham, 77
Etwall, Derby, 127
Exeter, Devon, St Leonard's, 119
Exton, Rutland, 61, 62

Fairford, Glouces., 102, 104
Farnacres, Durham, 29
Fledborough, Notts., 82, 126
Fleet, Lincs., 75
Fotheringhay, Northants., 28, 37, 118
Fowey, Cornwall, 75
Frampton, Lincs., 61
Frating, Essex, 124
Fressingfield, Suffolk, 108
Frome Selwood, Som., 45

Geddington, Northants., 120, 121
Gedney, Lincs., 60, 65
Gisburn, Yorks., 11
Gloucester, cathedral, 8
Grantham, Lincs., 24, 25, 31, 34, 42, 49, 61, 65, 71, 72, 74, 89, 95, 96, 109, 116, 122, 123, 127
Gretton, Northants., 92
Grinton, Yorks., 30

Haccombe, Devon, 28
Hale, Great, Lincs., 56
Hallaton, Leices., 25, 97
Halsall, Lancs., 84, 89
Harringworth, Northants., 88
Hawstead, Suffolk, 93
Hawton, Notts., 82, 88, 123, 124, 125
Heckington, Lincs., 82, 85, 89, 124
Hedon, Yorks., 30, 79
Hereford, cathedral, 34
Hereford, Little, Heref., 114, 116

Heslerton, West, Yorks., 79
Hessle, Yorks., 30
Hexham, Northumb., priory church, 4, 35
Hickleton, Yorks., 117
Higham Ferrers, Northants., 28, 37, 66, 90, 97, 105, 118
Hitchin, Herts., 33
Hodgeston, Pembroke, 85
Hooton Pagnell, Yorks., 59
Hough-on-the-Hill, Lincs., 53
Houghton-le-Spring, Durham, 78, 79
Hubberholm, Yorks., 116
Hull, Yorks., Holy Trinity, 30 ·
Hungerton, Leices., 36, 68
Hythe, Kent, 96

Immingham, Lincs., 64
Irstead, Norfolk, 108
Islip, Northants., 88

Jarrow-on-Tyne, Durham, St Paul's, 4

Kelmarsh, Northants., 130
Kenton, Devon, 110
Kettering, Northants., 62, 66, 100, 101
Ketton, Rutland, 66
Kewstoke, Som., 35
Keyston, Hunts., 66
Kirkburn, Yorks., 56
Kirkby in Malhamdale, Yorks., 11, 12
Kirkby Wiske, Yorks., 82

Langton, East, Leices., 83
Lapford, Devon, 108, 114
Lastingham, Yorks., 96
Launcells, Cornwall, 108
Lavenham, Suffolk, 70, 87, 90

Lawford, Essex, 80
Leeds, Yorks., St John's, 129
Leicester, St Mary's in the Castle, 65
Leigh, South, Oxon., 100
Leighton Buzzard, Beds., 33
Leverington, Cambs., 59
Lichfield, Staffs., cathedral, 81
Liddington, Rutland, 101
Lincoln, cathedral, 9, 10, 16, 34
Lindisfarne, Northumb., 5
Llananno, Radnor, 115
Llanbedr-ystrad-yw, Brecon, 102, 117
Llanegryn, Merioneth, 115
Llanelieu, Brecon,. 116, 117
Llanfair-ar-y-bryn, Carmarthen, 74
Llanfihangel-cwm-du, Brecon, 74
Llanrhaiadr-yn-Cynmerch, Denbigh, 104
Llanwnog, Montgom., 114, 115
Llywel, Brecon, 74, 115
London, old St Paul's, 80; St James Garlickhithe, 26; St Martin in the Fields, 130; St Mary-le-Strand, 130
Louth, Lincs., 32, 33, 62
Lowick, Northants., 104
Lowthorpe, Yorks., 26, 27, 37
Ludlow, Salop, 31, 34, 48, 110, 118, 121
Luffenham, North, Rutland, 85
Luton, Beds., 33, 108

Madley, Heref., 96
March, Cambs., 94
Margaretting, Essex, 60
Melford, Long, Suffolk, 34, 36
Melton Mowbray, Leices., 67
Middleham, Yorks., 28

Mitford, Northumb., 78
Monkwearmouth, Durham, 4, 5, 53
Montgomery, 114, 115
Morpeth, Northumb., 93

Nantwich, Cheshire, 84, 110
Navenby, Lincs., 82, 124
Newark-on-Trent, Notts., 81, 35, 42, 65, 96, 116, 126
Newport, Salop, 28
Newton Nottage, Glamorgan, 74
Norbury, Derby, 75, 84, 104
Northampton, All Saints', 32
Northleach, Glouces., 105
Northwold, Norfolk, 126
Norton-on-Tees, Durham, 52
Norwich, Norfolk, cathedral, 8, 118; St Peter Mancroft, 90
Nottingham, St Mary's, 32, 118

Oadby, Leices., 64
Oakham, Rutland, 61
Oswestry, Salop, 50
Othery, Som., 94
Othona; *see* Bradwell-juxta-Mare
Ottery St Mary, Devon, 118
Oundle, Northants., 62, 66, 96
Owston, Yorks., 126
Oxford, Merton college chapel, 39

Patricio, Brecon, 115
Patrick Brompton, Yorks., 82, 84
Patrington, Yorks., 62, 82, 83, 84, 99
Peterborough, Northants., cathedral, 4, 5, 6
Pickering, Yorks., 100, 104
Pleshy, Essex, 28
Pool, South, Devon, 70, 71, 126, 127

Preen, Salop, 93
Preston-in-Holderness, Yorks., 30

Quenington, Glouces., 67

Ramsey, Hunts., abbey church, 6
Ranworth, Norfolk, 106, 112
Raskelf, Yorks., 68
Rauceby, Lincs., 61
Raunds, Northants., 66, 89, 100, 104
Ripon, Yorks., cathedral, 4
Rochester, Kent, cathedral, 4
Romaldkirk, Yorks., 82
Ropsley, Lincs., 114
Rotherham, Yorks., college of Jesus, 25
Rothwell, Northants., 96
Rushden, Northants., 66, 90
Rushton, Northants., 90

St Breage, Cornwall, 100
St Michael Penkivel, Cornwall, 38, 73
St Neot, Cornwall, 104
St Peter's on the Wall; see Bradwell-juxta-Mare
St Winnow, Cornwall, 104
Salisbury, Wilts., cathedral, 49 ; St Thomas, 101
Sall, Norfolk, 73, 87, 111
Sampford, Great, Essex, 80
Sandiacre, Derby, 78, 84
Sawley, Derby, 90
Scarborough, Yorks., 42
Scawton, Yorks., 76, 128
Sedgefield, Durham, 129
Selby, Yorks., abbey church, 17
Sherburn-in-Elmet, Yorks., 35
Sherston Magna, Wilts., 36
Shrewsbury, Salop, St Chad's, 104; St Mary's, 104

Sibthorpe, Notts., 22, 26, 37, 82, 126
Skipwith, Yorks., 55
Skirlaugh, South, Yorks., 30, 105
Sleaford, Lincs., 61
Sneinton, Notts., 118
Snettisham, Norfolk, 67
Sompting, Sussex, 61
Southwell, Notts., cathedral, 81
Southwold, Suffolk, 106
Spalding, Lincs., 13, 14, 32
Spondon, Derby, 127
Stainfield priory, Lincs., 11
Stamford, Lincs., St Mary's, 31
Stanion, Northants., 121
Stebbing, Essex, 80
Stoke-by-Nayland, Suffolk, 87
Stony Stratford, Bucks., 33
Stottesdon, Salop, 36
Stratford-on-Avon, Warwicks., 32, 66
Stratton Strawless, Norfolk, 36
Sutton, King's, Northants., 67
Sutton, Long, Lincs., 32, 60, 89
Swymbridge, Devon, 114

Tamworth, Staffs., 29
Tanfield, West, Yorks., 128
Tansor, Northants., 56, 73, 90, 109, 118, 119, 123
Tattershall, Lincs., 28
Terrington St John's, Norfolk, 74
Tewkesbury, Glouces., abbey church, 35
Thaxted, Essex, 33, 73
Thirsk, Yorks., 96
Tickhill, Yorks., 63
Tideswell, Derby, 84, 90
Tilney All Saints, Norfolk, 60
Tilty, Essex, 80
Tong, Salop, 28
Totnes, Devon, 115

Trull, Som., 108
Trunch, Norfolk, 91, 108
Tugby, Leices., 58, 59
Tunstead, Norfolk, 87, 117, 128
Twywell, Northants., 127
Tydd St Giles, Cambs., 75

Ufford St Mary, Suffolk, 106

Wakefield, Yorks., cathedral, 35
Walpole St Peter, Norfolk, 86, 87, 88, 93, 118, 119
Walsingham, Little, Norfolk, 108
Walsoken, Norfolk, 60
Walton, West, Norfolk, 60, 75
Warmington, Northants., 109
Warwick, St Mary's, 97
Wath, Yorks. (North Riding), 89
Weaverthorpe, Yorks., 58
Well, Yorks., 107
Wellingborough, Northants., 88
Wells, Som., St Cuthbert's, 105
Wenhaston, Suffolk, 117
Wenlock priory, Salop, 93
Wensley, Yorks., 91
Westborough, Lincs., 88

Westbury-on-Trym, Glouces., 29, 47
Weston-in-Gordano, Som., 111, 114
Whaplode, Lincs., 60
Willingham, Cambs., 88
Winchester, Hants., cathedral, 6, 8, 34
Witham, North, Lincs., 76, 77
Witney, Oxon., 36
Wolborough, Devon, 109
Wolverhampton, Staffs., 29, 110
Woodborough, Notts., 83
Woodleigh, Devon, 126, 127
Worcester, cathedral, 34
Worstead, Norfolk, 105, 111
Wrexham, Denbigh, 47
Wymondham, Norfolk, 126

Yarmouth, Great, Norfolk, 42
York, cathedral, 85; St Mary's abbey, 85; All Saints', North Street, 104; St William's college, 25
Ythanceaster; *see* Bradwell-juxta-Mare

www.ingramcontent.com/pod-product-compliance
Ingram Content Group UK Ltd.
Pitfield, Milton Keynes, MK11 3LW, UK
UKHW042145280225
455719UK00001B/122